T0193697

What Is the Condition of Your Heart According To The Scriptures?

Roger Nimmo

WESTBOW
PRESS®
A DIVISION OF THOMAS NELSON
& ZONDERVAN

This book is a work of non-fiction. Unless otherwise noted, the author and the publisher make no explicit guarantees as to the accuracy of the information contained in this book and in some cases, names of people and places have been altered to protect their privacy.

Scripture taken from the King James Version of the Bible.

WestBow Press books may be ordered through booksellers or by contacting:

WestBow Press
A Division of Thomas Nelson & Zondervan
1663 Liberty Drive
Bloomington, IN 47403
www.westbowpress.com
1 (866) 928-1240

Because of the dynamic nature of the Internet, any web addresses or links contained in this book may have changed since publication and may no longer be valid. The views expressed in this work are solely those of the author and do not necessarily reflect the views of the publisher, and the publisher hereby disclaims any responsibility for them.

Any people depicted in stock imagery provided by Getty Images are models, and such images are being used for illustrative purposes only. Certain stock imagery © Getty Images.

ISBN: 978-1-9736-6707-0 (sc)
ISBN: 978-1-9736-6706-3 (hc)
ISBN: 978-1-9736-6708-7 (e)

Library of Congress Control Number: 2019908525

Print information available on the last page.

WestBow Press rev. date: 07/11/2019

Table of Contents

Endorsement

I believe the revelations that Roger has shared in this book are extremely valuable to anyone who wants to live a victorious Christian life.

These revelations have dramatically changed the way I consider my lifestyle. I realize now that what I allow or do not allow in my heart through what I watch on TV, movies, read, or listen to affects what I treasure in my heart. Being aware of this keeps my focus on Jesus instead of circumstances around me or what is happening in the world.

I strongly believe this book can help anyone with a teachable heart live a more successful Christian life.

God bless and enjoy!
Luann Nimmo

Introduction

(Please note that when the word man is used most of the time in scripture and in this book, it is referring to male and female, or humankind.)

Let us discuss Hebrews 4:11–16 and Hebrews 3:8–14.

> Let us labour therefore to enter into that rest, lest any man fall after the same example of unbelief. For the word of God is quick, and powerful, and sharper than any twoedged sword, piercing even to the dividing asunder of soul and spirit, and of the joints and marrow, and is a discerner of the thoughts and intents of the heart. Neither is there any creature that is not manifest in his sight: but all things are naked and opened unto the eyes of him with whom we have to do. Seeing then that we have a great high priest, that is passed into the heavens, Jesus the Son of God, let us hold fast our profession. For we have not an high priest which cannot be touched with the feeling of our infirmities; but was in all points tempted like as we are, yet without sin. Let us therefore come boldly unto the throne of grace, that we may obtain mercy, and find grace to help in time of need. Hebrews 4:11–16)

Harden not your hearts, as in the provocation, in the day of temptation in the wilderness: When your fathers tempted me, proved me, and saw my works forty years. Wherefore I was grieved with that generation, and said, They do alway err in their heart; and they have not known my ways. So I sware in my wrath, They shall not enter into my rest.) Take heed, brethren, lest there be in any of you an evil heart of unbelief, in departing from the living God. But exhort one another daily, while it is called To day; lest any of you be hardened through the deceitfulness of sin. For we are made partakers of Christ, if we hold the beginning of our confidence stedfast unto the end. (Hebrews 3:8–14)

Over the years, I have heard from most Christians that we are to do or respond to things or people from the heart. What if we have a heart hardened to God? What if we have an evil heart of unbelief? What if our hearts have treasured bad things? Should we still go with our hearts? Verse 12 in the passage from Hebrews above, "Take heed, brethren, lest there be in any of you an evil heart of unbelief, in departing from the living God," tells us that Christians can have evil hearts of unbelief. We cannot enter our rest or rely on our hearts if we harden our hearts or have evil hearts of unbelief. The soul is the gateway to what goes in and out of the heart. I believe the heart, soul, and spirit are very closely related.

I believe the scriptures teach that our spirits are made perfect by one offering.

But ye are come unto mount Sion, and unto the city of the living God, the heavenly Jerusalem, and to an innumerable company of angels, To the general assembly and church of the firstborn, which are written in heaven, and to God the Judge of all, and to the spirits of just men made perfect (Hebrews 12:22–23)

By the which will we are sanctified through the offering of the body of Jesus Christ once for all ... For by one offering he hath perfected for ever them that are sanctified. (Hebrews 10:10, 14)

Our spirit joined with the power of the Holy Spirit in our hearts should be the dominant force or factor in our lives. But if worldly garbage is allowed to flow into our hearts from our minds or senses, it will hinder the potential power in our hearts. We must always watch over or guard what we allow into our hearts. Impure hearts will restrict the power of the Holy Spirit and will lead us to the wrong destiny.

Hebrews 4:11 tells us to labor to have rest, which sounds strange. If we are not putting the Word into our hearts daily, we can fall into unbelief. Verse 12 gives us the answer for one part of entering that rest in our hearts—by putting the Word of God in our hearts. This part is a major part but not the only thing we are to do.

The Word is a discerner of the thoughts and intents of the heart. The next few verses explain we have a high priest, so we hold fast to our profession (our words are critical here for life and death). We are to come boldly to the throne of grace to obtain mercy and grace.

We access grace by faith, but our faith is restricted by hardened hearts and unbelief. We as Christians should never feel we cannot come boldly to the throne of grace. We come not because we have earned a right to come; we come not because we have been good and have not sinned lately. We come because Jesus intercedes for us. It pleases our Father if we come and receive His kingdom that He has freely given us by His grace.

From Hebrews 4:12, we get some understanding of how the Word works in and between the spirit, soul, body, and heart.

The children of Israel who came out of Egypt hardened their hearts and provoked God in the day of temptation in the wilderness. In the same way, Christians can provoke God, harden their hearts, tempt God, err in their hearts, and have evil hearts of unbelief; they will not be able to enter God's rest or reach God's destiny for their lives.

Hebrews 3:12 says, "Take heed, brethren, lest there be in any of you an evil heart of unbelief, in departing from the living God." The writer is calling them brethren, so they must have been Christians.

My understanding from the scriptures is that the condition of our hearts, or what we treasure in our hearts, will determine our victory in life; it will determine if we are more than conquerors. It will determine whether the power of the Holy Spirit is released from our hearts.

The Bible says that because we are His sons, God sent the Spirit of His Son into our hearts crying, "Abba, Father!" Galatians 4:6 says that the love of God has been shed abroad in our hearts by the Holy Spirit, which is given to us (Romans 5:5).

The heart is like a conduit for the power of the Holy Spirit to flow out from us to the world. Unbelief in our hearts can work in the opposite direction and void the faith in our hearts. Jesus said that if we had faith the size of a mustard seed, we would tell the mountain to be removed and it would be cast into the sea.

The Bible teaches us that we can have faith and doubt in our hearts at the same time. Our goal is to keep the good treasure in our hearts and keep the bad treasure out. How we can do it is what this book is all about.

In the King James Bible, the words *heart* and *hearts* are used over 900 times. The words are used over 170 times in the New Testament.

Matthew (19 times)
Mark (14)
Luke (23)
John (8)
Acts (24)
Romans (15)
1 Corinthians (5)
2 Corinthians (14)

Why I Wrote This Book

I have been a Christian since April 30, 1971. For the twenty-nine years before I learned many of the godly principles I cover in this book, my relationship with God was a roller-coaster—up and down going from strong faith to doubting God.

I began to see how important it was to understand God's love for me, the grace He gives me, and the power of His Word in my heart. I began to understand the power of my words and that I had to keep doubt and unbelief out of my heart. I learned that the righteousness of God in Christ is a gift from God, and never earned or lost by my good or bad behavior. When I learned to rightly divide His Word, my life underwent a great transformation.

After learning these truths, my roller-coaster life ceased, and life began to look more like a steady climb in the fruit and power of the Holy Spirit. I have learned how not to conform to the world's mind-set but to be transformed by renewing my mind by His Word.

Many Christians have not entered the rest God desires for them. Though they are born again as new creations in Christ and have received the gift of righteousness, they still act like the natural man spoken of in 1 Corinthians 2:14; the things of the Spirit are foolishness to them.

Once we are born again, we are no longer common or ordinary, and that should be obvious to everyone around us.

> For ye are yet carnal: for whereas there is among you envying, and strife, and divisions, are ye not carnal, and walk as men? (1 Corinthians 3:3)

> Let us labour therefore to enter into that rest, lest any man fall after the same example of unbelief. For the word of God is quick, and powerful, and sharper than any twoedged sword, piercing even to the dividing asunder of soul and spirit, and of the joints and marrow, and is a discerner of the thoughts and intents of the heart. (Hebrews 4:11–12)

We must labor to enter the rest God desires for us by meditating on the Word day and night and allowing it to discern the thoughts and intents of our hearts.

One major revelation I want to get across in this book is the relationship between the spirit, soul, heart, and body. The heart is a major part of the equation, but I have heard little teaching about that. For years I have studied what the Bible says about the relationship between the spirit, soul, heart, body, and the Word of God, and this is something the body of Christ needs to understand; it is a major revelation that will transform many Christian lives.

> Keep thy heart with all diligence; for out of it are the issues of life. (Proverbs 4:23)

CHAPTER 1

Spirit, Soul, Body, and Heart

For the word of God is quick, and powerful, and sharper than any twoedged sword, piercing even to the dividing asunder of soul and spirit, and of the joints and marrow, and is a discerner of the thoughts and intents of the heart.

The above verse shows us that man is composed of four parts. One part that has been often neglected is the heart. Let's try to define each and show how each is related to the others.

Man Is a Spirit

The spirit is the immaterial part of humans along with the soul and heart. Because these are immaterial, they are hard for us to understand. Some theologians believe the heart and the spirit are the same. Approximately 5 percent of the time in scripture, that might appear to be true. I believe from my study that the spirit and the heart are totally different identities. The born-again spirit is perfected forever while the heart fluctuates throughout our lives.

In the first chapter of Genesis, we read that man was created in the image and likeness of God. God created man from the dust of the ground and breathed His life into his nostrils, and man became a living soul. Here, we can see that man has material and immaterial aspects. Our spirits are eternal. Originally, it was God's will that we not die or depart from our physical bodies. When Jesus returns, we will receive immortal and incorruptible bodies.

Since God is a Spirit, man is a spirit. When Adam sinned, all creation was cursed. Corruption set in, and the correct relationship was broken between his spirit and God's Spirit.

By dying on the cross, Jesus provided the way for man's spirit to be born again (John 3). We each become one spirit with the Lord. If a person is born again, his or her spirit is made perfect (Hebrews 12:23, 10:14).

The scriptures below verify each of us is a spirit.

Acts 7:59
And they stoned Stephen, calling upon God, and saying, Lord Jesus, receive my spirit. ()

Acts 17:16
Now while Paul waited for them at Athens, his spirit was stirred in him, when he saw the city wholly given to idolatry. ()

Romans 1:9
For God is my witness, whom I serve with my spirit in the gospel of his Son, that without ceasing I make mention of you always in my prayers. ()

Romans 8:16 KJV
The Spirit itself beareth witness with our spirit, that we are the children of God. ()

And the very God of peace sanctify you wholly; and I pray God your whole spirit and soul and body be preserved blameless unto the coming of our Lord Jesus Christ. (1 Thessalonians 5:23)

The spirit of a man *is* the lamp of the Lord, Searching all the inner depths of his heart. (Proverbs 20:27)

To the general assembly and church of the firstborn, which are written in heaven, and to God the Judge of all, and to the spirits of just men made perfect. (Hebrews 12:23)

Man Lives in a Body

For us to live on this planet, we must have bodies, which give us a legal right to be on earth. Our bodies are subject to decay and corruption, but one day, we will put on incorruption and immortality. At the present, our spirits, souls, and hearts are in our bodies, our material part.

The human body is the most complex material system in the universe. One scientist stated that just one cell in the human body is more complex than all the machines and devices humankind has ever created. And we are supposed to believe what secular scientists tell us, that humankind just came about by time and chance over billions and billions of years? The odds against that occurring is the number one followed by five thousand zeros. Even in twenty thousand billion years, it would not happen. All natural systems always move from more-complex states to less-complex states when left to themselves.

For Jesus to save mankind from sin, He had to be born in the likeness of sinful man (Romans 8:3; Philippians 4:7).

Man Has a Soul

Most of the time, the soul is defined as the mind, will, and emotions. Our souls are considered immaterial. It is believed that animals have souls but not spirits. The word *soul* is used 498 times in the King James Version including 55 times in the New Testament.

Man Has a Heart

In a certain Bible dictionary of the Old Testament, the word *heart* means the "entire disposition of the *inner person*, mind, and *seat of emotions.*" In the New Testament, the word *heart* means "thoughts or feelings, analogy to middle, seat of understanding, *the seat and center of circulation*, seat of desires, feelings, affections, passions, impulses."

My own definition of the heart is the seat, place, or inner self that treasures what we have allowed there through our souls (mind, will, emotions). It is the place where the Word of God is permanently written. It contains the Spirit of God. What we store in our hearts will determine our destiny. The heart is the place where good or evil characteristics of man are stored. The condition of the heart will determine our victory in every area of our lives. This is the place of man God looks upon and judges the most. It is the middle part that links our soul to our spirit.

> But when the fulness of the time was come, God sent forth his Son, made of a woman, made under the law, To redeem them that were under the law, that we might receive the adoption of sons. And because ye are sons, God hath sent forth the Spirit of his Son into your hearts, crying, Abba, Father. (Galatians 4:4–6)

Summary

Only by the Word of God can we really understand the spirit, soul, and heart. They are closely intertwined in us and hard to separate. I'm not going to pretend I have this all figured out, but I believe we Christians are spirits perfected by God because we believe that Jesus died for our sins and that God raised Jesus from the dead. We receive and confess Him as Lord and Savior. We are one spirit with the Lord, and our spirits now have eternal life.

When we became born again, our spirits became one with the Lord, but we still have the same body, heart (but cleaned), and soul that are being transformed. We communicate with the world around us with the mind and our five senses. Our souls are the gates to our heart, so they are connected to each other. Any thought, idea, emotion, feeling, desire, affection, passion, or impulse may, after some time, be transferred from the mind and seated in the heart.

When we are born again, we receive cleaned-up hearts. Jesus said that we were cleansed by the Word He gave us. Most of the time, new Christians notice a major change in their emotions, feelings, desires, and so on. As time passes, the condition of our hearts depends on what we treasure in our hearts and what we give our attention to. Do we give more attention to the world or to the Word of God?

The Fruit of Your Life

> For a good tree bringeth not forth corrupt fruit; neither doth a corrupt tree bring forth good fruit. For every tree is known by his own fruit. For of thorns men do not gather figs, nor of a bramble bush gather they grapes. A good man out of the good treasure of his heart bringeth forth that which is good; and an evil man out of the evil treasure of his heart bringeth forth that which is evil: for

of the abundance of the heart his mouth speaketh. (Luke 6:43–45)

If we put the Word of God in our hearts, we will produce the fruits of righteousness or the fruit of the Spirit, and our hearts will be transformed along with our minds from glory to glory into the image of God.

Now the Lord is that Spirit: and where the Spirit of the Lord is, there is liberty. But we all, with open face beholding as in a glass the glory of the Lord, are changed into the same image from glory to glory, even as by the Spirit of the Lord. (2 Corinthians 3:17–18)

The Word says in Peter1:3 "His Divine Power has given unto us all things that pertain unto life and godliness through the knowledge of Him who has called us unto His glory and virtue." Does this mean these things are brought about in our lives automatically? No. We have been given a great inheritance, but it is up to us to find out what it is and receive His grace by faith (Romans 5:1–2). We are not saved by works of righteousness, but once we are saved by faith in Jesus Christ, we should eventually produce fruits of righteousness. The condition of our hearts will determine how much fruit we produce.

CHAPTER 2

Are Christians in America Trained More by the Word of God or the Word of Man?

Secular humanism is the belief that humanity is capable of morality and self-fulfillment without believing in God. The US Supreme Court established secular humanism as the state's religion. In all public schools and most universities in the United States, the assumption is that man can explain how everything came into being by time and chance without God.

Science today is based on the philosophy of materialism, the idea that all that exists is matter and energy. The rule of science means that every scientific explanation must start with this assumption, but it is just an assumption. I don't have a problem with this in real science or operational science. This is the science that has produced all the technology that has made our lives more comfortable, healthier, faster, easier, more efficient, securer, and many times more dangerous. Now through technology, we have the power to quickly destroy the world.

The other kind of science, if you want to call it that, is called origin or historical science. This kind of science sidesteps real science, which is based on direct observation, repeatable experiments, verification, and falsification. Of course there is a tremendous amount of evidence for changes that have taken place in the heavens, earth, and in living things. When we look at these natural changes, 99 percent of them are degeneration changes. On the genetic level, we never see information that has not existed before. The only changes we see are mutations in genes that already exist. Scientists have never observed new genes or new gene systems formed by time and chance. These so-called scientists just make up stories about what happened long, long ago and far, far away that can't be observed, tested, or repeated.

It's sad to say, but the world and many Christians as well have bought into these stories told by secular scientists. Many trust they know what they are talking about, take what they say about what happened long ago and far away, and reinterpret the scriptures to fit the latest scientific theory.

> And be not conformed to this world: but be ye transformed
> by the renewing of your mind, that ye may prove what
> is that good, and acceptable, and perfect, will of God.
> (Romans 12:2)

We have come to the point that most Christians believe man more that they believe God.

Behavioral science would make us believe nerve-racking is normal under certain circumstances; they say it is normal to be anxious and worried when certain things happen to us. Maybe for the natural man that is true, but not for children of God. We have in us the same power that raised Jesus from the dead.

> Now we have received, not the spirit of the world, but the
> spirit which is of God; that we might know the things
> that are freely given to us of God. Which things also we
> speak, not in the words which man's wisdom teacheth,
> but which the Holy Ghost teacheth; comparing spiritual

things with spiritual. But the natural man receiveth not the things of the Spirit of God: for they are foolishness unto him: neither can he know them, because they are spiritually discerned. But he that is spiritual judgeth all things, yet he himself is judged of no man. For who hath known the mind of the Lord, that he may instruct him? but we have the mind of Christ. (1 Corinthians 2:12–16)

Read: Romans 8:1–11

I understand this sounds very strange to many Christians because they often have too much unbelief in their hearts. The secular humanistic education they have received can contribute to this unbelief.

If the Word of God is seated in our hearts more than the world is, it will discern our hearts in what is the correct behavior and confession should be in our daily lives. I believe the condition of our hearts will determine our responses in every situation. In 2 Corinthians 2:14, we read that we should thank God, who always causes us to triumph in Christ. If we are Christians, God is not condemning us for anything, but He does expect us to grow up. Christianity is a life of constant growth from glory to glory.

Now the Lord is that Spirit: and where the Spirit of the Lord is, there is liberty. But we all, with open face beholding as in a glass the glory of the Lord, are changed into the same image from glory to glory, even as by the Spirit of the Lord. (2 Corinthians 3:17–18)

For our light affliction, which is but for a moment, worketh for us a far more exceeding and eternal weight of glory; While we look not at the things which are seen, but at the things which are not seen: for the things which

are seen are temporal; but the things which are not seen
are eternal. (2 Corinthians 4:17–18)

If you are getting a science education from the world, the assumption is
that all that exists is matter (things that can be seen) and energy (forces whose
effects can be naturally observed). If you are not prepared for the secular
humanistic indoctrination taught in school, your heart will often be flooded
with unbelief. If you don't understand that what is seen was created by what
is not seen, you will have a predominantly naturalistic understanding.

What we see is temporal; what we do not see is eternal. With a
naturalistic mind-set, things of the Spirit will seem foolish to us and we
will remain baby Christians. We must put God's Word, the truth, in our
hearts daily; by doing that, our hearts will focus on God and His Word.

> In the beginning was the Word, and the Word was with
> God, and the Word was God. The same was in the
> beginning with God. All things were made by him; and
> without him was not any thing made that was made. In
> him was life; and the life was the light of men. And the
> light shineth in darkness; and the darkness comprehended
> it not. (John 1:1–5)

The Word Became Flesh

> He was in the world, and the world was made by him, and
> the world knew him not. He came unto his own, and his
> own received him not. But as many as received him, to
> them gave he power to become the sons of God, even to
> them that believe on his name: Which were born, not of
> blood, nor of the will of the flesh, nor of the will of man,
> but of God. And the Word was made flesh, and dwelt

among us, (and we beheld his glory, the glory as of the only begotten of the Father,) full of grace and truth. And of his fulness have all we received, and grace for grace. For the law was given by Moses, but grace and truth came by Jesus Christ. No man hath seen God at any time, the only begotten Son, which is in the bosom of the Father, he hath declared him. (John 1:10–18)

For God so loved the world, that he gave his only begotten Son, that whosoever believeth in him should not perish, but have everlasting life. (John 3:16)

By whom also we have access by faith into this grace wherein we stand. (Romans 5:2)

For if by one man's offence death reigned by one; much more they which receive abundance of grace and of the gift of righteousness shall reign in life by one, Jesus Christ. (Romans 5:17)

Once I learned many of these truths, I began to reign in life as a king reigns through Jesus Christ. My life was much more consistent and peaceful, and I had less of the weight of sin, which did so easily beset me. I constantly looked to Jesus, the author and finisher of my faith (Hebrews 12:1–2).

During my roller-coaster years, I looked at myself—my good and bad works—being very conscious of my sin and not sufficiently conscious of Jesus. I thought I was as righteous as I acted. I thought God was dealing with me for my sin; I did not understand that righteousness was a gift from God. All my righteousness is as filthy as rags. I was too focused on how much I seemed to love Jesus rather than how much He loved me. The apostle John in the gospel of John referred to himself as the disciple Jesus loved.

The Lord hath appeared of old unto me, saying, Yea, I have loved thee with an everlasting love: therefore with lovingkindness have I drawn thee. (Jeremiah 31:3)

Should Christians always Have a Biblical Worldview?

The main principle I want to address in the book is the importance of understanding the condition of the heart. Many ministers say repeatedly, "We are a spirit, we have a soul, and we live in a body"; this is very good and something we need to know. Understanding how the condition of our hearts affects us in relationship with the soul, spirit, and body is very important as well, but that is left out of many sermons when it should be much of the focus.

For the word of God is quick, and powerful, and sharper than any twoedged sword, piercing even to the dividing asunder of soul and spirit, and of the joints and marrow, and is a discerner of the thoughts and intents of the heart. (Hebrews 4:12)

Once we become Christians, we should always have a biblical worldview, but that will not happen by chance. We must be in the Word of God daily. As Christians, we operate in a different kingdom than the world does. If you as a Christian are learning from the world through its educational systems, media, arts, entertainment—TV, radio, Facebook, schools, the internet, and so on—your heart is being saturated with the world's principles. The Bible tells us to watch over our hearts with all diligence for out of them flows the issues of life (Proverbs 4:23). We must not be conformed to this world, but we must be transformed by the renewing of our minds (Romans 12:2).

God created everything; He knows the beginning from the end. His

Word is the foundation for everything we need to know about life and godliness.

I share in this book many things God has revealed to me that have empowered me to walk in greater peace, love, joy, healing, prosperity, victory, wisdom, and preservation so I could really know Him and the power of His resurrection.

CHAPTER 3

We Must Put the Word of God in Our Hearts

For this cause I bow my knees unto the Father of our Lord Jesus Christ, Of whom the whole family in heaven and earth is named, That he would grant you, according to the riches of his glory, to be strengthened with might by his Spirit in the inner man; That Christ may dwell in your hearts by faith; that ye, being rooted and grounded in love, May be able to comprehend with all saints what is the breadth, and length, and depth, and height; And to know the love of Christ, which passeth knowledge, that ye might be filled with all the fulness of God. Now unto him that is able to do exceeding abundantly above all that we ask or think, according to the power that worketh in us. (Ephesians 3:14–20)

My understanding of the above scripture is that we are strengthened by His Spirit in our inner selves, our hearts, where He dwells by faith. We must be rooted and grounded in love in our hearts. But first we need to meditate on how the Bible defines love (1 Corinthians 13).

After we have meditated on what love is, we can tell when we are walking in love or not. If that Word is in our hearts, it will rise up in us and correct us to repent or change our mind-set, to walk in love. In this way, we can see that what has been sown in our hearts will determine the power of God flowing into or out of our lives. We decide, not God, what we put in our hearts. This is a powerful principle of God that we must understand; if we do not, we will experience little victory in life.

A heart full of the truth and understanding of the Word will produce great victory in every area of our bodies, hearts, and souls. Here is an example. When a thought comes to me, because I have a sound heart, I will recognize if it lines up with the Word or not. If it lines up, I take it by saying it (Matthew 6:31). If it does not line up with the Word, I don't say it, so I don't take it.

Satan's main goal is to kill, steal, and destroy by trying to fill our hearts with lies and deception that are not the will of God. We must keep or watch over our hearts with all diligence.

> Keep thy heart with all diligence; for out of it are the issues of life. Put away from thee a froward mouth, and perverse lips put far from thee. Let thine eyes look right on, and let thine eyelids look straight before thee. Ponder the path of thy feet, and let all thy ways be established. Turn not to the right hand nor to the left: remove thy foot from evil. (Proverbs 4:23–27)

God leads us, but He doesn't force us to follow or do His will. And we have the choice to not meditate on the Word of God; we are free to do as we please. We can hang around with the world if we like. We can keep doing what we did before we were born again and never pray, read the Word, or go to church. In this process, our hearts will become defiled again and may become worse than they were before we were saved. If we were truly saved but still practiced a sinful life style, that would produce grief and sorrow, but we are still the righteousness of God in Christ Jesus. God still loves us, and he is not condemning us. Of course, practicing a sinful lifestyle can produce catastrophic consequences.

This is where so many Christians have a problem; they wonder how anyone could be the righteousness of God in Christ but still sin. Let me ask some questions. Before you were saved, did your good works make you righteous? After you became a Christian, did your bad deeds make you unrighteous? If you said yes to either of those questions, you are saying that righteousness is based on your works. Many people would have answered yes to one of these questions, but God's ways are just and righteous. He justifies the ungodly. We were made sinners by one man's disobedience, and we were made righteous by one man's obedience. To the natural man, this makes no sense. We are righteous only by faith in Jesus Christ.

> For my thoughts are not your thoughts, neither are your ways my ways, saith the Lord. (Isaiah 55:8)

> For as by one man's disobedience many were made sinners, so by the obedience of one shall many be made righteous. (Romans 5:19)

> For if by one man's offence death reigned by one; much more they which receive abundance of grace and of the gift of righteousness shall reign in life by one, Jesus Christ. (Romans 5:17)

> God has already given to us all things.

> For the eyes of the Lord run to and fro throughout the whole earth, to shew himself strong in the behalf of them whose heart is perfect toward him. (2 Chronicles 16:9)

God's desire is to show Himself strong on our behalf. It is His pleasure to give us His kingdom. Luke 12:32

Grace and peace be multiplied unto you through the knowledge of God, and of Jesus our Lord, According as his divine power hath given unto us all things that pertain unto life and godliness, through the knowledge of him that hath called us to glory and virtue: Whereby are given unto us exceeding great and precious promises: that by these ye might be partakers of the divine nature, having escaped the corruption that is in the world through lust. (2 Peter 1:2–4)

This is one scripture I have meditated on quite often. It is our responsibility to multiply the grace and peace of God to us. This multiplication of grace and peace comes from our knowledge of God and of Jesus our Lord.

Only be thou strong and very courageous, that thou mayest observe to do according to all the law, which Moses my servant commanded thee: turn not from it to the right hand or to the left, that thou mayest prosper withersoever thou goest. This book of the law shall not depart out of thy mouth; but thou shalt meditate therein day and night, that thou mayest observe to do according to all that is written therein: for then thou shalt make thy way prosperous, and then thou shalt have good success. Have not I commanded thee? Be strong and of a good courage; be not afraid, neither be thou dismayed: for the Lord thy God is with thee whithersoever thou goest. (Joshua 1:7–9)

God told this to Joshua while he was under the law. How much better promises have we been given than Joshua received. We need to get up every morning and meditate on the Word, spend time in His presence, worship Him, and give Him praise and thanksgiving before we leave home. That will give us that attitude to be strong and very courageous. We need our bodies, minds, souls, and hearts to be aligned with the Spirit so we will be ready to be more than conquerors.

> These things have I spoken unto you, being yet present with you. But the Comforter, which is the Holy Ghost, whom the Father will send in my name, he shall teach you all things, and bring all things to your remembrance, whatsoever I have said unto you. Peace I leave with you, my peace I give unto you: not as the world giveth, give I unto you. Let not your heart be troubled, neither let it be afraid. (John 14:25–27)

The Holy Spirit is always with us to comfort, teach, remind us what Jesus said, and lead us in the way we should go. He never condemns us even if we mess up badly. Jesus has given us His peace. It is not like the peace the world gives, but we must not let our hearts be troubled or afraid. We always have a choice to let or not let our hearts be glad, deceived, full of love, joy, at peace, in doubt, in belief, assured, fearful, or whatever else we let in. We can take or not take a thought by saying or not saying it.

When I start having ungodly thoughts about people that cause unrest in my heart, as soon as I can, I get off by myself and just worship, praise God, speak His promises, and pray in the Holy Spirit; that brings my heart and mind back into the peace of God. The worst thing I could do would be to voice to someone all those bad thoughts I had about him or her or anyone else.

> For where envying and strife is, there is confusion and every evil work. (James 3:16)

This is not a message of condemnation. We don't need to condemn ourselves, because God is not, or focus on the bad condition of our hearts, or become sin-conscious all the time. What we need is more revelation of Jesus. We should spend more time in the presence of God with praise and thanksgiving, and He will empower us with His grace to live the victorious life he has called us to live.

Now, when I sin or miss the mark, I don't run from God; I run to Him with praise and thanksgiving because He has made me the righteousness of God in Christ Jesus. I believe God hates sin because it may bring harm to us. He runs to us, so to speak, encouraging us that Jesus paid for all our sins (2 Corinthians 5:21).

Sadly, many Christians think it is a good idea to focus on their sins. Jesus saved us from our sins (John 3:17). He did not come to condemn the world but to save us from our sins and the penalty for our sins. This is what the gospel is all about; it reveals God's righteousness. We are made righteous by faith in Jesus Christ, not by works (Romans 1:16–17).

What Is the Immaterial Human Heart?

In the Old Testament, the word *heart* according to *Strong's Hebrew Dictionary of the Old Testament* means the entire disposition of the inner person, mind, and seat of emotions.

In the New Testament, the word *heart* according to *Strong's Greek Dictionary of the New Testament* means thoughts or feelings analogous of the middle part of ourselves, the seat of understanding, the seat and center of circulation, the seat of desires, feelings, affections, passions, and impulses.

My definition of the heart is as a storage place or conduit which holds, or seats the Spirit. The place that stores the good or evil our minds have focused on. The place where God looks on and discerns our inner selves. It is the middle part that connects the soul and the spirit and a place of more-permanent storage of faith and or doubt that can restrict or release the power of the Holy Spirit out of us to the world.

I listed Old and New Testament scriptures of the heart that I thought would help us understand how the condition of our hearts will determine how much victory we will experience in everything that pertains to our life and godliness.

The following is a list of the functions, conditions, or operations of the heart described in scripture. I believe Christians and non-Christians alike can have hearts that could be in a good, bad, or even an evil condition. This list is not complete.

Table A

- evil thoughts of the heart
- deceived heart
- gladness of heart
- God's word in our hearts
- God looks on the heart
- prepared heart
- an understanding heart
- joy in our hearts
- peace in our hearts
- love in our hearts
- belief in our hearts
- doubt in our hearts
- rejoice in our hearts
- madness in our hearts
- evil heart of unbelief
- idols in our heart
- purposed in our hearts
- pure heart
- strengthened heart
- double heart
- fixed heart
- perverse heart
- wicked heart

- adultery in our hearts
- backslider in heart
- purified heart
- Holy Spirit in our hearts
- condemned heart
- written on the heart
- table of the heart
- proceed out of the heart, good or evil
- secrets of the heart
- God tests the heart
- counsels of the heart
- with the heart believe unto righteousness
- hidden person or man of the heart
- said in our heart
- assured heart
- out of the mouth proceeds that which fills the heart
- sown in the heart
- fearful of heart
- troubled heart
- hardened heart
- defiled heart

Here are things to do or keep in our hearts.

- Assure our hearts before God.
- Believe God in our hearts.
- Purify our hearts.
- Prepare our hearts.
- Rejoice in our hearts.
- Put God's Word in our hearts.
- Fix our hearts on God.
- Purpose in our hearts to walk by faith.

- Have Jesus-centered hearts.
- Strengthen our hearts.
- Keep understanding hearts.
- Keep living water flowing out of our hearts.
- Let love, joy, and peace flow from our hearts.

Here are things not to do or keep in our hearts.

- evil
- unbelief
- strife
- fear
- self-righteousness
- condemnation
- doubts about God
- perverseness
- hardness
- idolatry
- sin-consciousness
- troubles
- unbelief

Old Testament Scriptures about the Heart

Study these thirty-nine scriptures in context with the verses that precede and follow them and with all scripture.

- Genesis 6:5: Every imagination of the thoughts of his heart was only evil continually.
- Exodus 35:35: Them hath he filled with wisdom of heart.
- Deuteronomy 6:6: And these words, shall be in thine heart.

- Deuteronomy 11:16: Take heed to yourselves, that your heart be not deceived.
- Deuteronomy 20:8: And the officers shall speak further unto the people, and they shall say, What man is there that is fearful and fainthearted? let him go and return unto his house, lest his brethren's heart faint as well as his heart.
- Deuteronomy 28:47: Because thou serve not the Lord thy God with joyfulness, and with gladness of heart.
- Deuteronomy 30:14: But the word is very nigh unto thee, in thy mouth, and in thy heart (and Romans 10:8).
- 1 Samuel 2:1: And Hannah prayed, and said, My heart rejoiceth in the Lord.
- 1 Samuel 16:7: But the Lord said unto Samuel, Look not on his countenance, or on the height of his stature; because I have refused him: for the Lord seeth not as man seeth; for man looketh on the outward appearance, but the Lord looketh on the heart.
- 1 Kings 11:2: For surely they will turn away your heart after their gods.
- 1 Kings 11:4: When Solomon was old, that his wives turned away his heart after other gods: and his heart was not perfect with the Lord his God, as was the heart of David his father.
- 1 Chronicles 22:19: Now set your heart and your soul to seek the Lord your God.
- 2 Chronicles 12:14: And he did evil, because he prepared not his heart to seek the Lord.
- Ezra 7:10: For Ezra had prepared his heart to seek the law of the Lord, and to do it, and to teach in Israel statutes and judgments.
- Nehemiah 2:12: And I arose in the night, I and some few men with me; neither told I any man what my God had put in my heart.
- Job 22:22: Receive, I pray thee, the law from his mouth, and lay up his words in thine heart.

- Job 38:36: Who hath put wisdom in the inward parts? or who hath given understanding to the heart?
- Ecclesiastes 5:20: For he shall not much remember the days of his life; because God answereth him in the joy of his heart.
- Ecclesiastes 8:11: Because sentence against an evil work is not executed speedily, therefore the heart of the sons of men is fully set in them to do evil.
- Ecclesiastes 9:3: This is an evil among all things that are done under the sun, that there is one event unto all: yea, also the heart of the sons of men is full of evil, and madness is in their heart while they live, and after that they go to the dead.
- Ecclesiastes 9:3: This is an evil among all things that are done under the sun, that there is one event unto all: yea, also the heart of the sons of men is full of evil, and madness is in their heart while they live, and after that they go to the dead.
- Isaiah 57:15: For thus saith the high and lofty One that inhabiteth eternity, whose name is Holy; I dwell in the high and holy place, with him also that is of a contrite and humble spirit, to revive the spirit of the humble, and to revive the heart of the contrite ones.
- Isaiah 59:13: In transgressing and lying against the Lord, and departing away from our God, speaking oppression and revolt, conceiving and uttering from the heart words of falsehood.
- Jeremiah 7:24: But they hearkened not, nor inclined their ear, but walked in the counsels and in the imagination of their evil heart.
- Jeremiah 17:1: The sin of Judah is written with a pen of iron, and with the point of a diamond: it is graven upon the table of their heart.
- Jeremiah 17:9: The heart is deceitful above all things, and desperately wicked: who can know it?
- Jeremiah 24:7: And I will give them an heart to know me, that I am the Lord: and they shall be my people, and I will be their God: for they shall return unto me with their whole heart.

- Jeremiah 29:13: And ye shall seek me, and find me, when ye shall search for me with all your heart.
- Jeremiah 31:33: But this shall be the covenant that I will make with the house of Israel; After those days, saith the Lord, I will put my law in their inward parts, and write it in their hearts; and will be their God, and they shall be my people.
- Ezekiel 3:10: Moreover he said unto me, Son of man, all my words that I shall speak unto thee receive in thine heart, and hear with thine ears.
- Ezekiel 11:19: And I will give them one heart, and I will put a new spirit within you; and I will take the stony heart out of their flesh, and will give them an heart of flesh.
- Ezekiel 14:3: Son of man, these men have set up their idols in their heart, and put the stumblingblock of their iniquity before their face.
- Ezekiel 16:30: How weak is thine heart, saith the Lord God.
- Ezekiel 36:26: A new heart also will I give you, and a new spirit will I put within you: and I will take away the stony heart out of your flesh, and I will give you an heart of flesh (also Ezekiel 11:19).
- Daniel 1:8: But Daniel purposed in his heart that he would not defile himself with the portion of the king's meat, nor with the wine which he drank: therefore he requested of the prince of the eunuchs that he might not defile himself.
- Daniel 10:12: Then said he unto me, Fear not, Daniel: for from the first day that thou didst set thine heart to understand, and to chasten thyself before thy God, thy words were heard, and I am come for thy words.
- Daniel 11:27: And both of these kings' hearts shall be to do mischief.
- Malachi 4:6: And he shall turn the heart of the fathers to the children, and the heart of the children to their fathers, lest I come and smite the earth with a curse.

CHAPTER 4

What Are You Treasuring in Your Heart?

I believe the condition of our hearts will determine how much power of God will work in our lives. The state of our hearts does not affect how much God loves or sees us. God sees us perfect in Christ Jesus, but it will affect how we see God.

Blessed are the pure in heart for they shall see God (Matthew 5:8). God never condemns us but loves us unconditionally (Romans 8:1). The heart is filled with or affected by what we look at, people we hang out with, what we listen to, read, watch, say, study, learn and focus on.

When our hearts are like God's, the power of the Holy Spirit freely flows and is not restricted. Remember Galatians 4:6: God has sent forth the Spirit of His Son into your hearts crying, "Abba, Father!" If our hearts our defiled by unbelief, doubt, fear, or sin-consciousness, we restrict the power of the Holy Spirit. This occurs because the heart is like a conduit for the power of the Holy Spirit to flow out to our minds, bodies, souls, and all that God desires to do through us.

If we put the world in, we get the world out, which leads us to defeated lives and keeps us from entering His rest. Where our heart is, there is our treasure. What are you treasuring in your heart? Jesus said, "Where your treasure is, there will your heart be also." Matthew 12:35

reads, "A good man out of the good treasure of his heart brings forth good things: and an evil man out of the evil treasure brings forth evil things."

If you desire to bring good fruit from your life, you must treasure God and His Word in your heart.

Can Christians Have Evil Hearts of Unbelief?

> Wherefore (as the Holy Ghost saith, To day if ye will hear his voice, Harden not your hearts, as in the provocation, in the day of temptation in the wilderness: When your fathers tempted me, proved me, and saw my works forty years. Wherefore I was grieved with that generation, and said, They do alway err in their heart; and they have not known my ways. So I swore in my wrath, They shall not enter into my rest. Take heed, brethren, lest there be in any of you an evil heart of unbelief, in departing from the living God. (Hebrews 3:7–12)

In Hebrews 3:1–12, the writer uses the word *brethren*, so it's safe to say the writer was writing to fellow Christians. We are told to not let our hearts become hardened; we are to take heed lest we have evil heart of unbelief that departs from the living God. Yes, Christians can have evil hearts of unbelief. God forbid that these evil hearts should remain long or occur often.

From scripture, we know that it comes after God has spoken to us and we rebel or we refuse to accept the Word or to be obedient to what God has told us to do.

> Husbands, love your wives, even as Christ also loved the church, and gave himself for it. (Ephesians 5:25)

At one time in my marriage to my late wife, Denise, our relationship was struggling. All I could see was that it was all her fault. I complained to God about the terrible things I saw her do. I thought she was the problem; I thought I couldn't love her the way I should, but I thought I had a good excuse for that. God told me, *I didn't say you were to love her just when she acts right, or does right, or speaks right. Roger, you are to love her unconditionally as I love the church.* When I started to love her with an unconditional love, that changed our lives.

I wish I could say I was always obedient to the voice of God, but I wasn't. However, I have learned more and more over the years, and God has multiplied His grace and peace in my life through my knowledge of Him.

One of the most important revelations from God's Word we need in our lives is His grace toward us. I don't deserve God's grace, I can't earn God's grace, and I don't merit God's grace. If I think I can earn God's grace, I have become self-righteous, but my righteousness is a filthy rag.

> But we are all like an unclean *thing,* And all our righteousnesses *are* like filthy rags; We all fade as a leaf, And our iniquities, like the wind, Have taken us away. (Isaiah 64:6)

We never earn, deserve, or merit God's grace, but we can frustrate it or multiply it. We can frustrate it by thinking our good or bad deeds can change our righteousness with God.

We multiply God's grace by putting his Word in our hearts.

> I do not frustrate the grace of God: for if righteousness come by the law, then Christ is dead in vain. (Galatians 2:21)

> Grace and peace be multiplied unto you through the knowledge of God, and of Jesus our Lord, According as his divine power hath given unto us all things that pertain unto life and godliness, through the knowledge of him that

hath called us to glory and virtue: Whereby are given unto us exceeding great and precious promises: that by these ye might be partakers of the divine nature. (2 Peter 1:2–4)

I have learned that if a thought comes to me that doesn't line up with the Word, I do not take the thought by saying the thought (Matthew 6:21).

We must guard what enters our hearts. We are spirits with souls and hearts who occupy bodies. We are the guardians of our souls and hearts. Visions and thoughts go in both directions—from soul to heart and from heart to soul. What we allow our eyes to see, our ears to hear, and our mouths to speak enters our minds and can become fixed in our hearts. We have responsibility even for our thoughts; we should not let those thoughts contrary to the Word of God become seated in our hearts, because many of our thoughts come from the enemy. The thief comes not but for to steal, kill, and destroy (John 10:10).

We are to take every thought captive to the obedience of Christ. We do not want to associate with people who think it's always okay to speak their minds. If we don't have much Word in us, we will not know where the thought has come from. The last thing we should do is speak demonic thoughts even if they seem to be true. They are not the truth.

> For though we walk in the flesh, we do not war after the flesh: (For the weapons of our warfare are not carnal, but mighty through God to the pulling down of strong holds;) Casting down imaginations, and every high thing that exalteth itself against the knowledge of God, and bringing into captivity every thought to the obedience of Christ. (2 Corinthians 10:3–5)

We should have so much Word in us, that when a thought or an imagination comes that exalts itself against the knowledge of God, we take the thought captive to the obedience of Christ.

CHAPTER 5

How Is the Heart Related to Becoming Saved?

> But what saith it? The word is nigh thee, even in thy
> mouth, and in thy heart: that is, the word of faith, which
> we preach; That if thou shalt confess with thy mouth the
> Lord Jesus, and shalt believe in thine heart that God hath
> raised him from the dead, thou shalt be saved. For with
> the heart man believeth unto righteousness; and with
> the mouth confession is made unto salvation. For the
> scripture saith, Whosoever believeth on him shall not be
> ashamed. For there is no difference between the Jew and
> the Greek: for the same Lord over all is rich unto all that
> call upon him. For whosoever shall call upon the name
> of the Lord shall be saved. (Romans 10:8–12)

First, we must hear the Word; then, the word of faith Paul preached will be in our mouths and hearts. When we confess with our mouths Jesus as Lord and believe in our hearts that God raised him from the dead and are saved, we believe in our hearts unto righteousness and confess with our mouths unto salvation.

The heart and the soul are very closely linked; the soul is the gateway to the heart. What we hear sets in the heart; then, we believe the Word in our hearts and confess with our mouths that Jesus is Lord, and we are saved. This should be the way we live our Christian lives. We need to hear the Word every day, believe it, and confess it, which brings about our salvation. The word *salvation* means eternal life with Christ, peace of mind, preservation, deliverance, healing, and all the other exceedingly great and precious promises God has given us.

Remember that the soul is the mind, will, and emotions. Part of the mind is the senses. Many things may come to our mind. They could come up from the heart or from the senses.

> This is the covenant that I will make with them after those days, saith the Lord, I will put my laws into their hearts, and in their minds will I write them; And their sins and iniquities will I remember no more. Now where remission of these is, there is no more offering for sin. Having therefore, brethren, boldness to enter into the holiest by the blood of Jesus, By a new and living way, which he hath consecrated for us, through the veil, that is to say, his flesh; And having an high priest over the house of God; Let us draw near with a true heart in full assurance of faith, having our hearts sprinkled from an evil conscience, and our bodies washed with pure water. Let us hold fast the profession of our faith without wavering; (for he is faithful that promised. (Hebrews 10:16–23)

When the unsaved hear the Word of God, believe with their hearts, and confess with their mouths Jesus as Lord, they become saved, Jesus becomes their Lord, and they become the righteousness of God in Christ Jesus (Romans 10:8–10). Their hearts are washed clean, the Holy Spirit comes into their hearts, and they become a new creation in Christ (2 Corinthians 5:17), God's children and heirs. They receive the righteousness of God, their Father.

And because ye are sons, God hath sent forth the
Spirit of his Son into your hearts, crying, Abba, Father.
(Galatians 4:6)

Does this mean the heart stays forever clean and purified? No. An idea
in some Christian circles is that if a thought comes from the heart, it must be
good. I can give you many scriptures to show you that this is not scriptural.
I do believe that a person's heart is cleaned when he or she is first saved,
but we all can make the wrong choices, which may defile our hearts. From
my study, I would say over 50 percent of the verses in the New Testament
show the heart of a Christian could be filled with unbelief, hardened, full of
doubt, fearful, deceived, without understanding, darkened, and so on. This
is true for believers and nonbelievers alike. Read Hebrews 3–4.

Take heed, brethren, lest there be in any of you an evil
heart of unbelief, in departing from the living God. The
condition of our heart, results from the choices we make.
(Hebrews 3:12)

Should Christians Always Be Growing in Christ?

What an awesome salvation God has given to His children. We start
as babes, but we should increase in our maturity every day. We must watch
over or keep our hearts with all diligence because the issues of life flow
out of it (Proverbs 4:23). We must put the Word of God in our hearts daily
by reading, hearing, meditating on, and speaking the Word and laboring
to keep doubt and unbelief out of our hearts. We start our Christian
lives by hearing the Word of God and then believing in our hearts unto
righteousness and confessing with the mouth unto salvation. Every day,
we should hear, believe, speak, and receive this great salvation. With the
mouth, confession is made unto salvation. Read Romans 10:8–10.

So that thou incline thine ear unto wisdom, and apply thine heart to understanding. (Proverbs 2:2)

When wisdom entereth into thine heart, and knowledge is pleasant unto thy soul. Discretion will preserve you, understanding will keep you. (Proverbs 2:10–11)

Trust in the Lord with all thine heart; and lean not unto thine own understanding. (Proverbs 3:5)

He taught me also, and said unto me, Let thine heart retain my words: keep my commandments, and live. (Proverbs 4:4)

Let His words not depart from thine eyes; keep them in the midst of thine heart. For they are life unto those that find them, and health to all their flesh. Keep or watch over your heart with all diligence for out of it flow the issues of life. (Proverbs 4:21–23)

Jesus said, If ye continue in my word, then are ye my disciples indeed; And ye shall know the truth, and the truth shall make you free. (John 8:31–32)

As newborn babes, desire the sincere milk of the word, that ye may grow thereby. (1 Peter 2:2)

But whoso looks into the perfect law of liberty, and continues therein, he being not a forgetful hearer, but a doer of the work, this man shall be blessed in his deed. (James 1:25)

Can the Word of God we put in our hearts be choked with something else we put in our hearts? Yes.

> But Jesus answered and said, It is written, Man shall not
> live by bread alone, but by every word that proceeds out
> of the mouth of God. (Matthew 4:4)

Can We Have Unbelief and Faith at the Same Time in Our Hearts?

In Matthew 17:14–21, the disciples could not cast out a demon. When they asked Jesus why they could not, He told them it was because of their unbelief (v. 20). He did not say because of their lack of faith; He said, "If you have faith as a grain of mustard seed you could say unto this mountain be removed to yonder place and it would be removed and nothing would be impossible to you." In verse 21, He said, "but this kind goeth not out, but by prayer and fasting." The subject in verse 21 is unbelief. The only way to get rid of some kinds of unbelief is by prayer and fasting. Prayer and fasting have really helped me. I try to fast twice a year for five to seven days without eating solid food. I drink lots of water and a little juice. If you have not fasted for years, the first time you fast will be difficult. If you fast once or twice a year after that, it will be much easier. By learning to control our appetites, we learn to control our bodies. We must learn to tell our bodies what to do and not let our bodies rule us. Most people in America are ruled by food. Nearly 75 percent of American men and more than 60 percent of American women are obese or overweight.

Back to Matthew 17:14–21. The disciples had already been given authority over all the power of the enemy and to cast out demons (Matthew 10:7–8, 16:19). If the disciples had no faith, they would not have tried to cast the demon out to begin with.

All Christians have faith, but Hebrews 3:12 tells us that some brethren can have evil hearts of unbelief. This does not necessarily mean some are living in terrible sin; it just means they are not believing the truth of God in one or more areas of their lives.

There are at least three kinds of unbelief. One is ignorance, which means they just don't know or have never been taught right. Once they learn the truth, their ignorance is gone and so is their unbelief.

Another kind of unbelief is disbelief. This is when some have had wrong teaching in reference to the Bible. Maybe they were taught that God used sickness to teach us things. Once they have been shown by many scriptures that it is always God's will to heal them, their disbelief and thus their unbelief will be gone.

The last kind of unbelief is natural unbelief. This comes in from the senses. We have been trained to believe that what we see, hear, feel, and touch is more real than what God's Word says. Our senses are temporal while God is eternal.

Maybe we don't believe God has given us a great and awesome salvation, or we think we still have to be good and keep the law for God to bless us. I think even that is an evil heart of unbelief. Galatians tells us that those under the law are under the curse.

> For as many as are of the works of the law are under the
> curse: for it is written, Cursed is every one that continues
> not in all things which are written in the book of the law
> to do them. (Galatians 3:10)

I believe there are many instances when Christians have faith and unbelief or doubt in their hearts at the same time. Their doubts and their faith are working against each other, which hinders the power of God to flow from our hearts.

Hebrews 13:9 tells us that it is good that the heart is established by grace. If two equal forces act on the same object in opposite directions, no change in direction or movement occurs. This is why so many Christians miss it. They love God, are born again, go to church, tithe, read the Bible, and so on, but they are not seeing much victory in their lives. Their hearts are full of so many things that are hindering their faith. (See Table A).

It is not how much power we have in our lives but how much power we have going in the right direction, with the least resistance, at the right speed and in the right way. The Bible says we have the same power in us that raised Jesus from the dead. An electrical appliance hooked up to 220 volts has a lot of potential energy unless there is a short in the wires. A short is when the electrons don't move in the right direction or don't move along the right path. Whosoever shall say unto this mountain be removed and cast into the sea, and does not doubt in his heart, but shall believe that those things that he says shall come to pass he shall have whatsoever he says. Only Jesus had a perfect heart. We all miss it now and then. God is not condemning us, but His grace is sufficient for us, and His power is made perfect in our weaknesses.

> And these are they which are sown among thorns; such as hear the word, And the cares of this world, and the deceitfulness of riches, and the lusts of other things entering in, choke the word, and it becomes unfruitful. (Mark 4:18–19)

The above scripture tell us that the cares of the world, the deceitfulness of riches, and the lust for other things enter the heart and choke the Word, which becomes unfruitful. All Christians have faith in their hearts, but that faith may be choked by many things they have allowed to settle there.

CHAPTER 6

Does Righteousness Comes to Us Only by Faith in Jesus Christ?

The devil can steal from us if we think our good works make us righteous and our bad works make us unrighteous. I cannot lose the gift of righteousness by my bad works because I did not gain righteousness by them. I cannot become righteous by doing good, nor can I lose it by doing evil. God gives us the gift of righteousness through Jesus Christ, and so we receive all the good that Jesus deserves.

As Jesus became sin because He took our sin, we became righteous with Him because we received His righteousness. If our righteousness is not real, He did not take our sins when He died on the cross. When He became sin for us, we became righteous. He did not become sin by doing sin, so we don't become righteous by doing what's right. When He took our sins, He became cursed; when we become righteous, we are blessed. Jesus was not cursed because He deserved it, and neither are we blessed because we deserve it.

The Parable of the Sower

> And when much people were gathered together, and were
> come to him out of every city, he spake by a parable: A

sower went out to sow his seed: and as he sowed, some fell by the way side; and it was trodden down, and the fowls of the air devoured it. And some fell upon a rock; and as soon as it was sprung up, it withered away, because it lacked moisture. And some fell among thorns; and the thorns sprang up with it, and choked it. And other fell on good ground, and sprang up, and bare fruit an hundredfold. And when he had said these things, he cried, He that hath ears to hear, let him hear. And his disciples asked him, saying, What might this parable be? And he said, Unto you it is given to know the mysteries of the kingdom of God: but to others in parables; that seeing they might not see, and hearing they might not understand. (Luke 8:4–10)

The Parable of the Sower Explained

Now the parable is this: The seed is the word of God. Those by the wayside are the ones who hear; then the devil comes and takes away the word out of their hearts, lest they should believe and be saved. But the ones on the rock *are those* who, when they hear, receive the word with joy; and these have no root, who believe for a while and in time of temptation fall away. Now the ones *that* fell among thorns are those who, when they have heard, go out and are choked with cares, riches, and pleasures of life, and bring no fruit to maturity. But the ones *that* fell on the good ground are those who, having heard the word with a noble and good heart, keep *it* and bear fruit with patience. (Luke 8:11–15)

This parable teaches that even though we put the Word of God in our hearts, it can be choked by the cares, riches, and pleasures of life. The good ground mentioned is a noble and good heart that produces fruit. Producing fruit is easy when all the conditions are right, and we produce the right conditions when we enter God's rest in faith.

Many Christians think I'm crazy to say this, but when we stay under the law and stay sin-conscious, which brings condemnation on us, the result is unrest and no fruit. The Bible says it is a good thing that the heart be established with grace. Sinning or not sinning is not the issue as many ministers preach. Christians are not under sin, the penalty of sin, or the judgment of sin and should not have a mind-set that asks, Have I sinned? Do I need to confess that sin so I can be made righteous again?

I am so thankful that Jesus died for my past, present, and future sins. Obviously, there can be grievous consequences for living a sinful life. The root of this kind of lifestyle is unbelief, so we need to deal with that root.

Is My Heart Good Ground?

> The sower sows the word. And these are they by the way side, where the word is sown; but when they have heard, Satan cometh immediately, and taketh away the word that was sown in their hearts. And these are they likewise which are sown on stony ground; who, when they have heard the word, immediately receive it with gladness; And have no root in themselves, and so endure but for a time: afterward, when affliction or persecution arises for the word's sake, immediately they are offended. And these are they which are sown among thorns; such as hear the word, And the cares of this world, and the deceitfulness of riches, and the lusts of other things entering in, choke the word, and it becomes unfruitful. And these are they which are sown on good ground; such as hear the word,

and receive it, and bring forth fruit, some thirtyfold, some sixty, and some an hundred. (Mark 4:14–20)

Satan comes to take away the Word that was sown in their hearts. The condition of the heart will determine whether the Word produces fruit. If your heart is full of the cares of this world, deceit, riches, or the lust for other things, these things will choke the Word and keep it unfruitful. When you hear the Word and receive it in a pure heart of good ground, fruit is produced.

How can we tell if our hearts are good ground? Do we believe our righteousness is based on believing in Jesus or on our good works? Do we believe He has forgiven us of all our sins? Do we believe God's love for us is unconditional? Do we believe His will is for us to be whole and well? Do we believe He will condemn us if we sin? Do we believe He wants to bless us in every area of our lives? Do we believe God is always for us and not against us? Do we trust Him in everything? Have we interpreted certain scriptures incorrectly? Are we still living under the old covenant of law and not living under the gospel of grace?

How we answer these questions will give us some idea of the condition of our hearts. Do we have doubts in our hearts about God's love for us? Not every good and perfect gift from God? Do we have to do certain things to get God to forgive us? Do we lose our righteousness in Christ every time we sin? If we think these things are true, our confidence in God is very low and may be keeping us from producing much fruit. Not believing the truth about God causes us to distrust Him and rely on our own abilities.

Does the Word of God Clean Our Hearts?

Now ye are clean through the word which I have spoken unto you. Abide in me, and I in you. As the branch cannot bear fruit of itself, except it abide in the vine; no more can ye, except ye abide in me. I am the vine, ye are the branches: He that abideth in me, and I in him, the same bringeth forth much fruit: for without me ye can do nothing. If a man abide not in me, he is cast forth as a branch, and is withered; and men gather them, and cast them into the fire, and they are burned. If ye abide in me, and my words abide in you, ye shall ask what ye will, and it shall be done unto you. Herein is my Father glorified, that ye bear much fruit; so shall ye be my disciples. (John 15:3–8)

How did the disciples become clean by doing good things, by keeping the law, and by working for Jesus? None of our good works make us clean or righteous before God. Just like most things in life that must be cleaned often, so our hearts must be cleaned daily by the Word of God. By being in the Word, we abide in Him and bear much fruit. The fruit of ourselves is not good fruit. Christians as well as non-Christians can develop defiled hearts if they don't keep their hearts clean by the Word.

Not what goes into the mouth defiles a man; but what comes out of the mouth, this defiles a man. (Matthew 15:11)

Do not labor for the food which perishes, but for the food which endures to everlasting life, which the Son of Man will give you, because God the Father has set His seal on Him." Then they said to Him, "What shall we do, that we may work the works of God?" Jesus answered and said to them, "This is the work of God, that you believe in Him whom He sent." (John 6:27–29)

Hebrews 4:11–12 says we are to labor to enter His rest. It sounds strange to say labor to rest. This labor is easy, but we still have to discipline our flesh to take the time and do it. Hebrews 4:12 reads, "For the Word of

God is alive and active (powerful), and sharper than any twoedged sword, piercing even to the dividing of soul and spirit and the joints and marrow and is a discerner of the thoughts and intents of the heart."

We enter the rest by putting the Word in our hearts; it will discern the thoughts and intents of our hearts. Only the Word of God will reveal the condition of the heart. If you don't know the condition of your heart, you will have trouble keeping unbelief, hardness, darkness, doubts, idols, fears, and condemnation out of it.

Is your heart still hardened? Read Mark 8:13–21. The word *hardened* means to render insensitive, made hard, stupid, or callous. Jesus made disciples, and we have examples of Him correcting them. Jesus knew the condition of the heart of human beings. He knows the way mankind thinks. For Him to ask the question in Mark 8:17, He knew from the beginning that he had started with men who had hardened hearts. They were not born again until after He was raised from the dead. The more time He spent with them and teaching the Word to them, the less hardened their hearts became, except for Judas.

> The heart is deceitful above all things, and desperately wicked (added incurably sick): who can know it? (Jeremiah 17:9)

Jesus knew the condition of the hearts of man. The Word of faith purifies our hearts (Acts 15:9; James 4:7; 1 Peter 1:22). If the disciples had hardened hearts, we can as well. We must keep our hearts pure by putting the Word in our hearts every day and so enter His rest.

> This I say, therefore, and testify in the Lord, that you should no longer walk as the rest of the Gentiles walk, in the futility of their mind, having their understanding darkened, being alienated from the life of God, because of the ignorance that is in them, because of the blindness of

their heart; who, being past feeling, have given themselves over to lewdness, to work all uncleanness with greediness. But you have not so learned Christ, if indeed you have heard Him and have been taught by Him, as the truth is in Jesus: that you put off, concerning your former conduct, the old man which grows corrupt according to the deceitful lusts, and be renewed in the spirit of your mind, and that you put on the new man which was created according to God, in true righteousness and holiness. (Ephesians 4:17–24)

Paul was telling the Christians at Ephesus to no longer walk a certain way; we have a choice to walk or not walk as the Gentiles did. We have a choice to walk in the futility of our minds and have our understanding darkened because of ignorance and the blindness of our hearts. Every day, we must be renewed in the spirit of our minds so our hearts can be renewed according to God in true righteousness and holiness.

Many Christians including myself have been totally defeated because we didn't keep the Word in our hearts daily and keep out evil thoughts, deception, doubt, unbelief, idols, perversion, fear, hardness, strife, self-righteousness—the list goes on.

Guard, keep, and watch over your heart with all diligence. Don't take thoughts by speaking them if you know they are not godly thoughts.

Psalms—Scriptures of the Heart

Study these twenty-four scriptures in context with the verses that precede and follow them and with all scripture.

- Psalm 7:9: Oh let the wickedness of the wicked come to an end; but establish the just: for the righteous God trieth the hearts and reins.

- Psalm 10:13: Wherefore doth the wicked contemn God? he hath said in his heart, Thou wilt not require it.
- Psalm 12:2: They speak vanity every one with his neighbour: with flattering lips and with a double heart do they speak.
- Psalm 14:1: The fool hath said in his heart, There is no God. They are corrupt, they have done abominable works, there is none that doeth good.
- Psalm 16:9: Therefore my heart is glad, and my glory rejoiceth: my flesh also shall rest in hope.
- Psalm 17:3: Thou hast proved mine heart; thou hast visited me in the night; thou hast tried me, and shalt find nothing; I am purposed that my mouth shall not transgress.
- Psalm 19:8: The statutes of the Lord are right, rejoicing the heart: the commandment of the Lord is pure, enlightening the eyes.
- Psalm 19:14: Let the words of my mouth, and the meditation of my heart, be acceptable in thy sight, O Lord, my strength, and my redeemer.
- Psalm 24:3–4: Who shall ascend into the hill of the Lord? or who shall stand in his holy place? He that hath clean hands, and a pure heart; who hath not lifted up his soul unto vanity, nor sworn deceitfully. He shall receive the blessing from the Lord, and righteousness from the God of his salvation. This is Jesus.
- Psalm 27:3: Though an host should encamp against me, my heart shall not fear: though war should rise against me, in this will I be confident.
- Psalm 27:14: Wait on the Lord: be of good courage, and he shall strengthen thine heart: wait, I say, on the Lord.
- Psalm 32:11: Be glad in the Lord, and rejoice, ye righteous: and shout for joy, all ye that are upright in heart.
- Psalm 36:1: The transgression of the wicked saith within my heart, that there is no fear of God before his eyes.

- Psalm 37:4: Delight thyself also in the Lord: and he shall give thee the desires of thine heart.
- Psalm 37:31: The law of his God is in his heart; none of his steps shall slide.
- Psalm 53:1: The fool hath said in his heart, There is no God. Corrupt are they, and have done abominable iniquity: there is none that doeth good.
- Psalm 55:21: The words of his mouth were smoother than butter, but war was in his heart: his words were softer than oil, yet were they drawn swords.
- Psalm 57:7: My heart is fixed, O God, my heart is fixed: I will sing and give praise.
- Psalm 62:10: Trust not in oppression, and become not vain in robbery: if riches increase, set not your heart upon them.
- Psalm 78:8: And might not be as their fathers, a stubborn and rebellious generation; a generation that set not their heart aright, and whose spirit was not stedfast with God.
- Psalm 95:8: Harden not your heart, as in the provocation, and as in the day of temptation in the wilderness.
- Psalm 95:10: Forty years long was I grieved with this generation, and said, It is a people that do err in their heart, and they have not known my ways.
- Psalm 109:22: For I am poor and needy, and my heart is wounded within me.

CHAPTER 7

Explanations of New and Old Testament Scriptures on the Heart

And He left them, and getting into the boat again, departed to the other side. Now the disciples had forgotten to take bread, and they did not have more than one loaf with them in the boat. Then He charged them, saying, "Take heed, beware of the leaven of the Pharisees and the leaven of Herod." And they reasoned among themselves, saying, "*It is* because we have no bread." But Jesus, being aware of *it,* said to them, "Why do you reason because you have no bread? Do you not yet perceive nor understand? Is your heart still hardened? Having eyes, do you not see? And having ears, do you not hear? And do you not remember? When I broke the five loaves for the five thousand, how many baskets full of fragments did you take up?" They said to Him, "Twelve." "Also, when I broke the seven for the four thousand, how many large baskets full of fragments did you take up?" And they said, "Seven." So He said to them, "How *is it* you do not understand?" (Mark 8:13–21)

I want to expound on the last statement, "How is it you do not understand?" We Christians do not understand when our hearts become hardened. As I have said before, our minds are the gates to our hearts. Of course, all our senses work by the brain. We must be very diligent to guard our hearts by keeping watch over what we allow into our hearts through our senses. This is not easy because we live in a corrupt world. We are in the world and a light in the world, but not of the world. Wherever we are and whatever we do, we should walk in love and be a witness of Jesus Christ.

Before I leave the house every morning, I want my mind, heart, and body to be in the best condition to face the world. If possible, I prepare for each day, which starts the night before by getting enough sleep. I spend quality time in the Word and in prayer almost every morning. I eat a healthy breakfast. Sometimes it doesn't work out that way, but God's grace is sufficient for me; His power is made perfect in our weakness.

> Thou therefore, my son, be strong in the grace that is in Christ Jesus. And the things that thou hast heard of me among many witnesses, the same commit thou to faithful men, who shall be able to teach others also. Thou therefore endure hardness, as a good soldier of Jesus Christ. (2 Timothy 2:1–3)

The Disciples' Hearts were Hardened and Full of Unbelief

> Now when Jesus was risen early the first day of the week, he appeared first to Mary Magdalene, out of whom he had cast seven devils. And she went and told them that had been with him, as they mourned and wept. And they, when they had heard that he was alive, and had been seen of her, believed not. After that he appeared in another form unto two of them, as they walked, and went into the country. And they went and told it unto the residue:

neither believed they them. Afterward he appeared unto the eleven as they sat at meat, and upbraided them with their unbelief and hardness of heart, because they believed not them which had seen him after he was risen. (Mark 16:9–14)

It's amazing that though the disciples had spent three years with Jesus and witnessed miracles, they still had a place for unbelief and hardness in their hearts.

The Bible says it's impossible to please God without faith. Our hearts can become hardened when we don't consider what we are daily allowing into our hearts and focus on ungodly things; they become insensitive to God's power and grace. Some Christians love God, go to church, pay their tithes, and pray, but then they believe they can watch whatever they want on TV and don't think it affects their hearts. Watching TV is like inviting others into your home and having fellowship with them. Everything you see and hear on TV could eventually become seated in your heart; even the commercials motivate us to buy things we really don't need. Because there is so much bad news on TV, I know watching too much news is bad for my heart, so I have cut back on how much news I watch.

Be not deceived: evil communications corrupt good manners. (1 Corinthians 15:33)

Finally, brethren, whatsoever things are true, whatsoever things are honest, whatsoever things are just, whatsoever things are pure, whatsoever things are lovely, whatsoever things are of good report; if there be any virtue, and if there be any praise, think on these things. (Philippians 4:8)

If we think about anything long enough, it will be seated in our hearts, so we should think of true, honest, just, pure, lovely, respectful, virtuous, and praiseworthy things. Christians who dwell on negative things have divided hearts.

A Tree Is Known by Its Fruit

> For a good tree bringeth not forth corrupt fruit; neither doth a corrupt tree bring forth good fruit. For every tree is known by his own fruit. For of thorns men do not gather figs, nor of a bramble bush gather they grapes. A good man out of the good treasure of his heart bringeth forth that which is good; and an evil man out of the evil treasure of his heart bringeth forth that which is evil: for of the abundance of the heart his mouth speaketh. (Luke 6:43–45)

What Are We Treasuring in Our Hearts?

We and only we are responsible for the treasure of our hearts, not our pastors, parents, spouses, or friends. I believe that when we account for ourselves in heaven, it will all come down to the treasure in our hearts out of which flows the issues of life. Our good works and deeds do not make us righteous before God; if anything they are only the fruits of righteousness. The strong, unhindered faith in our hearts produces the fruits of righteousness.

> For whatsoever is born of God overcomes the world: and this is the victory that overcomes the world, even our faith. (1 John 5:4)

If you know things are not right in your life, I bet you'll find that it goes back to the treasure in your heart. Ask the Lord if your heart is the heart of God.

Lying to the Holy Spirit

> But a certain man named Ananias, with Sapphira his wife, sold a possession. And he kept back *part* of the proceeds, his wife also being aware *of it,* and brought a certain part and laid *it* at the apostles' feet. But Peter said, "Ananias, why has Satan filled your heart to lie to the Holy Spirit and keep back *part* of the price of the land for yourself? While it remained, was it not your own? And after it was sold, was it not in your own control? Why have you conceived this thing in your heart? You have not lied to men but to God." Then Ananias, hearing these words, fell down and breathed his last. So great fear came upon all those who heard these things. And the young men arose and wrapped him up, carried *him* out, and buried *him.* (Acts 5:1–6)

Satan got Ananias to lie to the Holy Spirit. Many sold their houses and property and gave the money to the apostles. Whatever their motive was, it made them look good in the eyes of the people. If our hearts are in the right condition, we would never give to impress others. John 5:44 asks, "How can you believe, which receive honor from one another, and seek not the honor that comes from God alone?" I think that Ananias was not a true believer and that he probably sought honor from men, not God. His heart must have been in horrible condition if Satan was allowed to convince him to lie to the Holy Spirit. Our number one goal in life is to please God; we need to walk in His love and be a blessing to as many people as we can. We must always strive to please God above man.

> Even as I please all men in all things, not seeking mine own profit, but the profit of many, that they may be saved. (1 Corinthians 10:33)

Paul tried to please men in all things not to make himself look good before men but that they might be saved.

> For do I now persuade men, or God? or do I seek to please men? for if I yet pleased men, I should not be the servant of Christ. (Galatians 1:10)

Paul's goal was not to seek to please men but to please God as the servant of God.

The Eyes of the Heart

> Cease not to give thanks for you, making mention of you in my prayers; That the God of our Lord Jesus Christ, the Father of glory, may give unto you the spirit of wisdom and revelation in the knowledge of him: The eyes of your understanding being enlightened; that ye may know what is the hope of his calling, and what the riches of the glory of his inheritance in the saints, And what is the exceeding greatness of his power to us-ward who believe, according to the working of his mighty power. (Ephesians 1:16–19)

If Christians' hearts are not in good condition, they won't see or understand the Word correctly. The Holy Spirit is in our hearts (Galatians 4:6). If our hearts are hardened with unbelief, strife, fear, condemnation, doubt, idols, perverseness, or sin-consciousness, the Holy Spirit can barely flow from the heart.

At times, all of us have given place to some of these things in our hearts. Remember that by the Word, we can clean and purify our hearts. Another good way is to pray in the Holy Spirit by praying in tongues.

Follow after charity, and desire spiritual gifts, but rather that ye may prophesy. For he that speaketh in an unknown tongue speaketh not unto men, but unto God: for no man understandeth him; howbeit in the spirit he speaketh mysteries. But he that prophesieth speaketh unto men to edification, and exhortation, and comfort. He that speaketh in an unknown tongue edifieth himself; but he that prophesieth edifieth the church. (1 Corinthians 14:1–4)

A great way I have found to edify myself is to pray in tongues. If I sense that my heart is full of a care that should not be there, I get off by myself, worship God, and pray in tongues. It is amazing how fast I can rid my heart of it and build myself up.

And now, brethren, I commend you to God, and to the word of his grace, which is able to build you up, and to give you an inheritance among all them which are sanctified. (Acts 20:32)

But ye, beloved, building up yourselves on your most holy faith, praying in the Holy Ghost. These two scriptures tell us we can build ourselves up by praying and hearing the Word of His grace. (Jude 1:20)

And on the morrow, when they were come from Bethany, he was hungry: And seeing a fig tree afar off having leaves, he came, if haply he might find any thing thereon: and when he came to it, he found nothing but leaves; for the time of figs was not yet. And Jesus answered and said unto it, No man eat fruit of thee hereafter for ever. And his disciples heard it. And they come to Jerusalem: and Jesus went into the temple, and began to cast out them that sold and bought in the temple, and overthrew the tables of the moneychangers, and the seats of them that sold doves.

And when even was come, he went out of the city. And in the morning, as they passed by, they saw the fig tree dried up from the roots. And Peter calling to remembrance saith unto him, Master, behold, the fig tree which thou cursed is withered away. And Jesus answering saith unto them, Have faith in God. For verily I say unto you, That whosoever shall say unto this mountain, Be thou removed, and be thou cast into the sea; and shall not doubt in his heart, but shall believe that those things which he saith shall come to pass; he shall have whatsoever he saith. (Mark 11:12–15, 19–23)

Much has been said about "whosoever shall say," which is very important. What I want to focus on is the condition of the heart before we say unto our mountain. It is easier to say something than to keep our hearts in the right condition and remove the doubts in our heart before we say it.

If before we say unto our mountain we have doubt, fear, unbelief, or any condition of the heart not right, that will affect the results. We have a lot of excuses for why the circumstances don't change, but seldom do we say it was because we had doubt in our hearts. We can have faith along with doubt and unbelief in our hearts; these forces work in opposite directions. I think we should examine what we hear, speak, watch, and read, the people we run around with, and what we learn in church and school that might cause our hearts to be in a negative condition. This restricts the power of God flowing out of our lives. Our good works are great and worth performing, but they are not enough to keep our hearts in the right condition for His Spirit and power to flow out of us.

Scriptures on the Heart in Proverbs

Study these thirty-one scriptures in context with the verses that precede and follow them and with all scripture.

- Proverbs 2:2: So that thou incline thine ear unto wisdom, and apply thine heart to understanding.
- Proverbs 2:10–11: When wisdom entereth into thine heart, and knowledge is pleasant unto thy soul. Discretion will preserve you, understanding will keep you.
- Proverbs 3:5: Trust in the Lord with all thine heart; and lean not unto thine own understanding.
- Proverbs 4:4: He taught me also, and said unto me, Let thine heart retain my words: keep my commandments, and live.
- Proverbs 4:21: Let His words not depart from thine eyes; keep them in the midst of thine heart.
- Proverbs 4:23: Keep thy heart with all diligence; for out of it are the issues of life.
- Proverbs 6:14: A worthless person, a wicked man has perverseness in his heart, he deviseth mischief continually; he soweth discord.
- Proverbs 7:2–3: Keep my commandments. Bind them upon thy fingers, write them upon the table of thine heart.
- Proverbs 7:10: And, behold, there met him a woman with the attire of an harlot, and crafty of heart.
- Proverbs 8:5: O ye simple, understand wisdom: and, ye fools, be ye of an understanding heart.
- Proverbs 10:20: The tongue of the just is as choice silver: the heart of the wicked is little worth.
- Proverbs 11:20: They that are of a froward heart are abomination to the Lord: but such as are upright in their way are his delight.
- Proverbs 12:8: A man shall be commended according to his wisdom: but he that is of a perverse heart shall be despised.

- Proverbs 12:20: Deceit is in the heart of them that imagine evil: but to the counsellors of peace is joy.
- Proverbs 12:23: A prudent man concealeth knowledge: but the heart of fools proclaimeth foolishness.
- Proverbs 14:14: The backslider in heart shall be filled with his own ways: and a good man shall be satisfied from himself.
- Proverbs 14:30: A sound heart is the life of the flesh: but envy the rottenness of the bones.
- Proverbs 15:7: The lips of the wise disperse knowledge: but the heart of the foolish doeth not so.
- Proverbs 15:13: A merry heart maketh a cheerful countenance: but by sorrow of the heart the spirit is broken.
- Proverbs 15:14: The heart of him that hath understanding seeketh knowledge: but the mouth of fools feedeth on foolishness.
- Proverbs 15:28: The heart of the righteous studieth to answer: but the mouth of the wicked poureth out evil things.
- Proverbs 16:1: The preparations of the heart in man, and the answer of the tongue, is from the Lord.
- Proverbs 16:5: Every one that is proud in heart is an abomination to the Lord: though hand join in hand, he shall not be unpunished.
- Proverbs 16:21: The wise in heart shall be called prudent: and the sweetness of the lips increaseth learning.
- Proverbs 16:23: The heart of the wise teacheth his mouth, and addeth learning to his lips.
- Proverbs 17:16: Wherefore is there a price in the hand of a fool to get wisdom, seeing he hath no heart to it?
- Proverbs 17:20: He that hath a froward heart findeth no good: and he that hath a perverse tongue falleth into mischief.
- Proverbs 17:22: A merry heart doeth good like a medicine: but a broken spirit drieth the bones.

- Proverbs 18:2: A fool hath no delight in understanding, but that his heart may discover itself.
- Proverbs 18:12: Before destruction the heart of man is haughty, and before honor is humility.
- Proverbs 18:15: The heart of the prudent getteth knowledge; and the ear of the wise seeketh knowledge.

CHAPTER 8
Old Testament Scriptures

Keep, Guard, Watch Over, your heart with all diligence;
for out of it are the issues of life. (Proverbs 4:23)

W e must diligently keep and watch our hearts. Are we discerning what we are allowing into our hearts? If a negative thought comes into our minds, we should take the thought captive to the obedience of Christ and cast away imaginations and every high thing that exalts itself against the knowledge of God. Don't say thoughts that are not godly or lovely. If a negative thought comes to your mind, speak something godly.

But I beseech you, that I may not be bold when I am present with that confidence, wherewith I think to be bold against some, which think of us as if we walked according to the flesh. For though we walk in the flesh, we do not war after the flesh: (For the weapons of our warfare are not carnal, but mighty through God to the pulling down of strong holds;) Casting down imaginations, and every high thing that exalts itself against the knowledge of God, and bringing into captivity every thought to the obedience of Christ. (2 Corinthians 10:2–5)

Walking in the flesh will defile our hearts; if we allow our hearts to become hardened, we will walk in the flesh. We should take control of our thoughts and not say thoughts that don't edify others—doing so could defile our hearts and others' as well. The soul is the gate to the heart; just because something enters our minds doesn't mean it will be seated in our hearts.

We don't need to condemn ourselves if we are not doing everything right because God is not condemning us. We should pray daily that God will lead us to listening to, reading, hearing, and learning the things that are good for the heart. We should focus on the Word of Christ, not the words of man. The TV shows we watch, the books we read, and the commercials we observe determine some of the conditions of the heart. The Word will discern the thoughts and intents of the heart. The Word will also show us how we allowed our hearts to get in the wrong condition to begin with.

> Wherefore I was grieved with that generation, and said, They do alway err in their heart; and they have not known my ways. So I sware in my wrath, They shall not enter into my rest. Take heed, brethren, lest there be in any of you an evil heart of unbelief, in departing from the living God. But exhort one another daily, while it is called To day; lest any of you be hardened through the deceitfulness of sin. (Hebrews 3:10–13)

> Solomon's wives turned away his heart after other gods. (1 Kings 11:4)

> But king Solomon loved many strange women, together with the daughter of Pharaoh, women of the Moabites, Ammonites, Edomites, Zidonians, and Hittites: Of the nations concerning which the Lord said unto the children

of Israel, Ye shall not go in to them, neither shall they come in unto you: for surely they will turn away your heart after their gods: Solomon clave unto these in love. And he had seven hundred wives, princesses, and three hundred concubines: and his wives turned away his heart. For it came to pass, when Solomon was old, that his wives turned away his heart after other gods: and his heart was not perfect with the Lord his God, as was the heart of David his father. (1 Kings 11:1–4)

Here is a good example of what can happen to our hearts when we surround ourselves with the wrong company. Our hearts may tend to turn away from God to idols. Of course, we have a better covenant than Solomon did, and we have the infilling of the Holy Spirit to help empower us if we choose to keep our hearts free from the contamination of this world.

It was never in God's heart for a husband to have more than one wife. God allowed the children of Israel many things that were not His perfect will; that was only because all creation was in a fallen corrupted state. Humanity's only hope was for Jesus coming in the flesh and dying for the sins of the human race.

Numbers 13 records Moses sending leaders from each of the twelve tribes to go into the Promised Land and spy out the land. They returned with pomegranates, figs, and a cluster of grapes so big that two of them had to carry it. Ten of the spies reported that the land was flowing with milk and honey. Then they gave an evil report—the children of Israel could not possess the land because the people there were strong and of great stature and the cities were walled and very big. They said they had seen the sons of Anak, who were giants, and the spies felt like grasshoppers compared to them. So ten of the spies discouraged the people from possessing the land. But Caleb said, "Let us go up at once for we are well able to possess it." The ten convinced the people that they wouldn't be able to take the land. The people murmured against Moses and Aaron; they wanted to return to Egypt.

New Testament Scriptures on the Heart

Study these thirty-six scriptures in context with the verses that precede and follow them and with all scripture.

- Matthew 5:8: Blessed are the pure in heart: for they shall see God.
- Matthew 5:28: But I say unto you, That whosoever looketh on a woman to lust after her hath committed adultery with her already in his heart.
- Matthew 6:21: For where your treasure is, there will your heart be also.
- Matthew 9:4: And Jesus knowing their thoughts said, Wherefore think ye evil in your hearts?
- Matthew 12:34: O generation of vipers, how can ye, being evil, speak good things? for out of the abundance of the heart the mouth speaketh.
- Matthew 12:35: A good man out of the good treasure of the heart bringeth forth good things: and an evil man out of the evil treasure bringeth forth evil things.
- Matthew 13:15: For this people's heart is waxed gross, and their ears are dull of hearing, and their eyes they have closed; lest at any time they should see with their eyes and hear with their ears, and should understand with their heart, and should be converted, and I should heal them.
- Matthew 13:19: When any one heareth the word of the kingdom, and understandeth it not, then cometh the wicked one, and catcheth away that which was sown in his heart. This is he which received seed by the way side.

- Matthew 15:18: But those things which proceed out of the mouth come forth from the heart; and they defile the man.
- Matthew 15:19: For out of the heart proceed evil thoughts, murders, adulteries, fornications, thefts, false witness, blasphemies.
- Matthew 22:37: Jesus said unto him, Thou shalt love the Lord thy God with all thy heart, and with all thy soul, and with all thy mind.
- Mark 3:5: And when he had looked round about on them with anger, being grieved for the hardness of their hearts, he saith unto the man, Stretch forth thine hand. And he stretched it out: and his hand was restored whole as the other.
- Mark 4:15: And these are they by the way side, where the word is sown; but when they have heard, Satan cometh immediately, and taketh away the word that was sown in their hearts.
- Mark 8:17: And when Jesus knew it, he saith unto them, Why reason ye, because ye have no bread? perceive ye not yet, neither understand? have ye your heart yet hardened?
- Mark 11:23: For verily I say unto you, That whosoever shall say unto this mountain, Be thou removed, and be thou cast into the sea; and shall not doubt in his heart, but shall believe that those things which he saith shall come to pass; he shall have whatsoever he saith.
- Mark 16:14: Afterward he appeared unto the eleven as they sat at meat, and upbraided them with their unbelief and hardness of heart, because they believed not them which had seen him after he was risen.
- Luke 1:51: He hath shewed strength with his arm; he hath scattered the proud in the imagination of their hearts.
- Luke 2:19: But Mary kept all these things, and pondered them in her heart.
- John 14:27: Jesus said "let not your heart be troubled, neither let it be afraid or fearful."

- Luke 6:45: A good man out of the good treasure of his heart bringeth forth that which is good; and an evil man out of the evil treasure of his heart bringeth forth that which is evil: for of the abundance of the heart his mouth speaketh.

- Luke 8:15: But that on the good ground are they, which in an honest and good heart, having heard the word, keep it, and bring forth fruit with patience.

- Luke 16:15: And he said unto them, Ye are they which justify yourselves before men; but God knoweth your hearts: for that which is highly esteemed among men is abomination in the sight of God.

- Luke 21:26: Men's hearts failing them for fear, and for looking after those things which are coming on the earth: for the powers of heaven shall be shaken.

- Luke 24:25: Then he said unto them, O fools, and slow of heart to believe all that the prophets have spoken.

- Luke 24:32: And they said one to another, Did not our heart burn within us, while he talked with us by the way, and while he opened to us the scriptures?

- Luke 24:38: And he said unto them, Why are ye troubled? and why do thoughts arise in your hearts?

- John 12:40: He hath blinded their eyes, and hardened their heart; that they should not see with their eyes, nor understand with their heart, and be converted, and I should heal them.

- John 14:1: Let not your heart be troubled: ye believe in God, believe also in me.

- John 16:22: And ye now therefore have sorrow: but I will see you again, and your heart shall rejoice, and your joy no man taketh from you.

- Acts 1:24: And they prayed, and said, Thou, Lord, which knowest the hearts of all men, shew whether of these two thou hast chosen.

- Acts 2:26: Therefore did my heart rejoice, and my tongue was glad; moreover also my flesh shall rest in hope.
- Acts 2:37: Now when they heard this, they were pricked in their heart, and said unto Peter and to the rest of the apostles, Men and brethren, what shall we do?
- Acts 5:3: But Peter said, Ananias, why hath Satan filled thine heart to lie to the Holy Ghost, and to keep back part of the price of the land?
- Acts 7:51: Ye stiffnecked and uncircumcised in heart and ears, ye do always resist the Holy Ghost: as your fathers did, so do ye.
- Acts 7:54: When they heard these things, they were cut to the heart, and they gnashed on him with their teeth.
- Acts 8:37: And Philip said, If thou believest with all thine heart, thou mayest. And he answered and said, I believe that Jesus Christ is the Son of God.

CHAPTER 9
Be of Good Cheer

The point I want to make with Numbers 13 is that when God tells us something in His Word, we should always believe and receive it. If we surround ourselves with people who discourage us with words of doubt and unbelief, our hearts will be full of unbelief and doubt, and that will prevent us from fulfilling God's destiny for our lives.

Don't associate with discouraging people any more than you have to. Be a person who always builds up the hearts of those around you. Be an encourager, not a discourager (Proverbs 18:21). Life and death are in the power of the tongue. Jesus said that a good man out of the good treasure of his heart would bring forth good things. If you want to bring forth good things from your heart, you must treasure good things in it.

Another huge principle that Christians must understand is that the condition of their hearts will determine how they see their circumstances. Christians can observe the same circumstances, but those with the heart of God will not be troubled by the adversity they see; they will be confident in victory by the power and grace of God. Their hearts will be fixed and flooded with light to see the way out (1 Corinthians 10:13). They have understanding hearts and know Jesus is always the way of escape. They know that God will not allow them to be tempted beyond what they are able to handle.

Christians with evil hearts of unbelief (Hebrews 3:12) will focus on the negative in their circumstances and their problems. They will confess what they see and not what God has given to them to overcome this world.

As long as we are in this body, there will be tribulation in life. The Bible is very plain on this subject. We live in a fallen, corrupted, futile, and decaying world that is passing away (Romans 8:18–21; 1 John 2:17).

Deceitfulness of Riches and the Lust for Other Things

Some people are deceived into believing that if they could just get to a certain point, life would be perfect; they think that if they earned enough money and had just the right education, spouse, and government, they would reach a utopia with no more trials and tribulations. This deception will lead to lives of repeated disappointments and will harden their hearts. Jesus said, "In the world, you shall have tribulation, but be of good cheer, I have overcome the world." We are to be of good cheer no matter what the circumstances may be. I know that sounds insane to most people; they think that we can't control our emotions, that they control us. Read what Jesus said in John 16 and remember what happened to Jesus and His disciples after that. A heart full of the Word and not the world will be a heart of courage and good cheer. Jesus said, "Man shall not live by bread alone, but by every word that proceeds out of the mouth of God."

> Jesus said "For what is a man profited, if he shall gain the whole world, and lose his own soul? or what shall a man give in exchange for his soul?" (Matthew 16:26)

Solomon, son of David, the king of Israel, was one of the richest men ever. His wealth today would be about $2 trillion. He had everything he wanted, everything that this world could offer, yet he said the following:

> So I was great, and increased more than all that were before me in Jerusalem: also my wisdom remained with me. And whatsoever mine eyes desired I kept not from them, I withheld not my heart from any joy; for my heart rejoiced in all my labour: and this was my portion of all my labour. Then I looked on all the works that my hands had wrought, and on the labour that I had laboured to do: and, behold, all was vanity and vexation (a state of being annoyed, frustrated, and worried) of spirit, and there was no profit under the sun. (Ecclesiastes 2:9–11)

God wants all His children to be prosperous and blessed, but He wants them always to seek the blesser and remember that riches are very deceitful; they will never get us to a utopia. Solomon started out with the heart of God but allowed the deceitfulness of riches and the lust for other things to enter him and choke the Word

Labor to Enter God's Rest

> Let us therefore fear, lest, a promise being left us of entering into his rest, any of you should seem to come short of it. For unto us was the gospel preached, as well as unto them: but the word preached did not profit them, not being mixed with faith in them that heard it. For we which have believed do enter into rest, as he said, As I have sworn in my wrath, if they shall enter into my rest: although the works were finished from the foundation of the world. (Hebrews 4:1–3)

> And he said, My presence shall go with thee, and I will give thee rest. (Exodus 33:14)

> Therefore my heart is glad, and my glory rejoices: my flesh also shall rest in hope. (Psalm 16:9)

If our hearts are glad, our bodies will rest in hope. A rested body is a body that's well and full of strength.

> Fret not thyself because of evildoers, neither be thou envious against the workers of iniquity. For they shall soon be cut down like the grass, and wither as the green herb. Trust in the Lord, and do good; so shalt thou dwell in the land, and verily thou shalt be fed. Delight thyself also in the Lord: and he shall give thee the desires of thine heart. Commit thy way unto the Lord; trust also in him; and he shall bring it to pass. And he shall bring forth thy righteousness as the light, and thy judgment as the noonday. Rest in the Lord, and wait patiently for him: fret not thyself because of him who prospers in his way, because of the man who brings wicked devices to pass. Cease from anger, and forsake wrath: fret not thyself in any wise to do evil. (Psalm 37:1–8)

If we fret or worry, we are not at rest. How many times will thoughts come to our minds that are not based on evidence? If we take the thought by speaking it and letting it settle in our hearts, we will lose our peace and cease to be at rest. We are instructed in the following scripture to do these things.

- Fret not.
- Trust in the Lord and do good.
- Delight in the Lord.
- Commit our ways to the Lord.
- Rest in the Lord.

- Wait patiently for Him.
- Cease from anger.
- Forsake wrath.

Most all of these things are done in the heart and soul, not the body, but they certainly affect the health of the body.

Are Christians Just Natural People?

> The life is more than meat, and the body is more than raiment. Consider the ravens: for they neither sow nor reap; which neither have storehouse nor barn; and God feeds them: how much more are ye better than the fowls? And which of you with taking thought can add to his stature one cubit? If ye then be not able to do that thing which is least, why take ye thought for the rest? Consider the lilies how they grow: they toil not, they spin not; and yet I say unto you, that Solomon in all his glory was not arrayed like one of these. If then God so clothe the grass, which is to day in the field, and to morrow is cast into the oven; how much more will he clothe you, O ye of little faith? And seek not ye what ye shall eat, or what ye shall drink, neither be ye of doubtful mind. For all these things do the nations of the world seek after: and your Father know that ye have need of these things. But rather seek ye the kingdom of God; and all these things shall be added unto you. Fear not, little flock; for it is your Father's good pleasure to give you the kingdom. (Luke 12:23–32)

The natural man thinks he must work hard to get what he needs, but Christians operate in a different kingdom that instructs us to rest in God's grace, His unearned, undeserved, and unmerited favor.

> There remains therefore a rest to the people of God. (Hebrews 4:9)

> For he that is entered into his rest, he also hath ceased from his own works, as God did from his. (Hebrews 4:10)

> Let us labour therefore to enter into that rest, lest any man fall after the same example of unbelief. (Hebrews 4:11)

It sounds crazy that we are to labor to have rest. How do we labor to enjoy His rest? What does the next verse say?

> For the word of God is quick, and powerful, and sharper than any twoedged sword, piercing even to the dividing asunder of soul and spirit, and of the joints and marrow, and is a discerner of the thoughts and intents of the heart. (Hebrews 4:12)

The Word of God in our hearts gives us that rest. His Word is life to those who find it and health to their flesh. The Word in our hearts does the work. I believe it pleases God more than anything for us, His children, to take from Him what He has given to us. It's our father's good pleasure to give us the kingdom. If He offers it, He wants us to take it. By taking from Him, we please and glorify Him. Grace supplies, but the law demands.

Does Our Unbelief Hinder the Power of God Flowing out of Our Lives?

And he went out from thence, and came into his own country; and his disciples follow him. And when the sabbath day was come, he began to teach in the synagogue: and many hearing him were astonished, saying, From whence hath this man these things? and what wisdom is this which is given unto him, that even such mighty works are wrought by his hands? Is not this the carpenter, the son of Mary, the brother of James, and Joses, and of Juda, and Simon? and are not his sisters here with us? And they were offended at him. But Jesus, said unto them, A prophet is not without honour, but in his own country, and among his own kin, and in his own house. And he could there do no mighty work, save that he laid his hands upon a few sick folk, and healed them. And he marvelled because of their unbelief. And he went round about the villages, teaching. (Mark 6:1–6)

Take heed, brethren, lest there be in any of you an evil heart of unbelief, in departing from the living God. (Hebrews 3:12)

So we see that they could not enter in because of unbelief. (Hebrews 3:19)

Seeing therefore it remains that some must enter therein, and they to whom it was first preached entered not in because of unbelief. (Hebrews 3:19)

> Let us labour therefore to enter into that rest, lest any man
> fall after the same example of unbelief. (Hebrews 4:11)

We can allow unbelief to enter our hearts in so many ways—wrong teachings, friends, music, associates, movies, where we go, our educational systems and even by thoughts of doubt we take by speaking them; the list goes on and on.

We allow many things that we should not allow. Satan gets inroads into our lives with our permission by what we allow into our lives. We alone are responsible for what we allow into our hearts. Jesus said,

> Let not your heart be troubled: ye believe in God, believe
> also in me. (John 14:1)

> Peace I leave with you, my peace I give unto you: not as
> the world giveth, give I unto you. Let not your heart be
> troubled, neither let it be afraid. (John 14:27)

> Submit yourselves therefore to God. Resist the devil, and
> he will flee from you. (James 4:7)

Satan seeks to devour us, but he can devour us only if we let him. The only authority Satan has over our lives is what we give him by what we believe and speak. Hebrews 2:14 says that through His death, Jesus destroyed the devil.

Satan's only weapon is deception; he is a liar, the father of all lies. We have been given authority over his power, so we must steadfastly resist him. Most of the time, we give him authority over ourselves by what we say. According to Proverbs 18:21, death and life are in the power of the tongue. God will never answer a prayer and do something for us that He has already given to us.

Be sober, be vigilant; because your adversary the devil, as a roaring lion, walks about, seeking whom he may devour: Whom resist stedfast in the faith, knowing that the same afflictions are accomplished in your brethren that are in the world. (1 Peter 5:8)

New Testament Scriptures on Unbelief

Study these sixteen scriptures in context with the verses that precede and follow them and with the rest of scripture.

- Matthew 13:58: And he did not many mighty works there because of their unbelief.
- Matthew 17:20: And Jesus said unto them, Because of your unbelief: for verily I say unto you, If ye have faith as a grain of mustard seed, ye shall say unto this mountain, Remove hence to yonder place; and it shall remove; and nothing shall be impossible unto you.
- Mark 6:6: And he marvelled because of their unbelief. And he went round about the villages, teaching.
- Mark 9:24: And straightway the father of the child cried out, and said with tears, Lord, I believe; help thou mine unbelief.
- Mark 16:14: Afterward he appeared unto the eleven as they sat at meat, and upbraided them with their unbelief and hardness of heart, because they believed not them which had seen him after he was risen.
- Romans 3:3: For what if some did not believe? Shall their unbelief make the faith of God without effect?
- Romans 4:20: He staggered not at the promise of God through unbelief; but was strong in faith, giving glory to God.

- Romans 11:20: Well; because of unbelief they were broken off, and thou stand by faith. Be not highminded, but fear.
- Romans 11:23: And they also, if they abide not still in unbelief, shall be grafted in: for God is able to graft them in again.
- Romans 11:30: For as ye in times past have not believed God, yet have now obtained mercy through their unbelief.
- Romans 11:32: For God hath concluded them all in unbelief, that he might have mercy upon all.
- 1 Timothy 1:13: Who was before a blasphemer, and a persecutor, and injurious: but I obtained mercy, because I did it ignorantly in unbelief.
- Hebrews 3:12: Take heed, brethren, lest there be in any of you an evil heart of unbelief, in departing from the living God.
- Hebrews 3:19: So we see that they could not enter because of unbelief.
- Hebrews 4:6: Seeing therefore it remains that some must enter therein, and they to whom it was first preached entered not in because of unbelief.
- Hebrews 4:11: Let us labour therefore to enter that rest, lest any man fall after the same example of unbelief.

CHAPTER 10

Is It Possible That 1 John 1:1–10 Was Not Written to Christians?

That which was from the beginning, which we have heard, which we have seen with our eyes, which we have looked upon, and our hands have handled, of the Word of life; (For the life was manifested, and we have seen it, and bear witness, and shew unto you that eternal life, which was with the Father, and was manifested unto us;) That which we have seen and heard declare we unto you, that ye also may have fellowship with us: and truly our fellowship is with the Father, and with his Son Jesus Christ. And these things write we unto you, that your joy may be full. This then is the message which we have heard of him, and declare (many translations use the word announce for declare which means "make a public formal declaration") unto you, that God is light, and in him is no darkness at all. If we say that we have fellowship with him, and walk in darkness, we lie, and do not the truth: But if we walk in the light, as he is in the light, we have fellowship one with another, and the blood of Jesus Christ his Son cleanses us from all sin. If we say that we have no sin, we deceive ourselves, and the truth is not in us. If we confess our sins, he is faithful and just to forgive us our sins, and to cleanse us from all unrighteousness. If we say that we have not sinned, we make him a liar, and his word is not in us. (1 John 1:1–10)

In my opinion, the above scripture cannot mean what so many Christians have been taught. Let me explain. The first chapter of 1 John does not refer to the readers as children. Chapters 2–5 refer to them as children nine times. In 1 John 2, we read of the Antichrist three times. Chapter 4 mentions the Antichrist once, and 2 John 1:7 mentions the Antichrist once. I believe that in the first chapter of 1 John the author was addressing Gnostics who had crept into the church and were spreading their ideas, but he desired fellowship with them by explaining to them that he was an eyewitness of the deity of Jesus Christ. Gnostics would fall into the category of Antichrists.

Gnosticism

Gnosticism was an idea that crept into the church during the first century. Gnostics believed that man was basically good but just trapped in an evil body. Sin was not an issue, only ignorance was. Gnosticism held that the Creator of the earth had been created by an even more supreme being, that the Creator of the earth had messed up and created all matter as evil. So then, it was all about knowledge. In 1 John 2–3, I see John warning the readers to consider if what they believe is the truth. He explained what truth, light, and darkness were and told them to keep God's Word in their hearts. He warned them to beware of Antichrists and their ideas.

Do Many Christians Live in Constant Condemnation because of Their Sins?

Many Christians interpret 1 John 1:9 to mean that if we sin, our fellowship with God is broken and He can't have fellowship with us until we confess that sin; He then forgives us and cleanses us from all unrighteousness.

The book of 1 John was written to a specific group of people. It is hard to understand a letter written by someone we don't know, meant for another person we don't know; we aren't aware of their relationship. Scripture must always be interpreted by scripture in the right context. We do not make a doctrine out of one verse when at least fifty other scriptures are giving us a totally different message. No other scripture implies that Christians must confess their sins to be forgiven and cleansed from all unrighteousness. When I sin, it does not cause God to break fellowship with me. I believe multiple scriptures teach us that I am not under the Law and that I am dead to sin. If I am dead to sin, I do not respond to it. All my past, present and future sins have been paid for by the blood of Jesus once for all time. There may be an issue in my life where I need to repent, or change my mind set. If I don't repent, it may cause harm to me or my family.

Under the new covenant, we are not under the Law, so sin is not imputed to us. Sin is not imputed when there is no Law. Remember that we are spirits with souls and hearts who live in bodies. My spirit is one with the Lord's.

> But ye are come unto mount Sion, and unto the city of the living God, the heavenly Jerusalem, and to an innumerable company of angels, To the general assembly and church of the firstborn, which are written in heaven, and to God the Judge of all, and to the spirits of just men made perfect. (Hebrews 12:22–23)

I am not perfect in my body, soul, or heart, but I am perfect in my spirit. God does not condemn us when we sin; "I am dead to sin and live unto righteousness" (1 Peter 2:24).

In 1 John 1–10, I see John trying to convince the reader of something he and many others saw, touched, heard, and bore witness of the Word Life. It appears that John had not had fellowship with them but wanted that. Read verse 7: if we are a Christians, we all have the Holy Spirit in us and are walking in the light as He is in the light. Even if it does not appear to us or others that we are, we still are walking in the light, because as He is, so are we in this world. 1 John 4:17

> Herein is our love made perfect, that we may have boldness in the day of judgment: because as he is, so are we in this world. There is no fear in love; but perfect love casteth out fear: because fear hath torment. He that fears is not made perfect in love. (1 John 4:17–18)

So many other scriptures in the New Testament speak otherwise. We do not lose our righteousness in Christ when we sin. There are more than fifty scriptures in the New Testament that mention forgiveness of sins, thy sins be forgiven, remission of sins, does not remember our sins, saved from our sins, sins may be blotted out, and washing away our sins, Jesus gave himself for our sins, being dead in your sins, himself purged our sins, once purged should have had no more consciousness of sins, and so on.

No other scripture in the New Testament tells us we have to confess our sins to be cleansed from unrighteousness. When Jesus died on the cross, He took the judgment for all man's sins past, present, and future for all time in His body. He was called the Lamb of God that took away the sins of the world. The only conditions are that we must believe with all our hearts that God raised Him from the dead and confess with our mouths that He is our Lord.

Here are just a few scriptures that support my understanding:

- Acts 5:31: Him hath God exalted with his right hand to be a Prince and a Saviour, for to give repentance to Israel, and forgiveness of sins.

- Acts 13:38: Be it known unto you therefore, men and brethren, that through this man is preached unto you the forgiveness of sins.

- Acts 26:18: To open their eyes, and to turn them from darkness to light, and from the power of Satan unto God, that they may receive forgiveness of sins, and inheritance among them which are sanctified by faith that is in me.

- Ephesians 1:7: In whom we have redemption through his blood, the forgiveness of sins, according to the riches of his grace.

- Colossians 1:14: In whom we have redemption through his blood, even the forgiveness of sins.

- John 1:29: The next day John sees Jesus coming unto him, and saith, Behold the Lamb of God, which taketh away the sin of the world.

- Romans 6:2: God forbid. How shall we, that are dead to sin, live any longer therein?

- Romans 6:11: Likewise reckon ye also yourselves to be dead indeed unto sin, but alive unto God through Jesus Christ our Lord.

- Romans 6:18: Being then made free from sin, ye became the servants of righteousness.

- Romans 8:2: For the law of the Spirit of life in Christ Jesus hath made me free from the law of sin and death.

- 2 Corinthians 5:21: For he hath made him to be sin for us, who knew no sin; that we might be made the righteousness of God in him.

- Hebrews 1:3: Who being the brightness of his glory, and the express image of his person, and upholding all things by the word of his power, when he had by himself purged our sins, sat down on the right hand of the Majesty on high.

- 1 Peter 2:24: Who his own self bare our sins in his own body on the tree, that we, being dead to sins, should live unto righteousness: by whose stripes ye were healed.

Is Jesus Our Savior from Our Past, Present, and Future Sins?

When Jesus died on the cross, all our sins were future sins. I challenge anyone to look at 1 John 1:1–10 in its context; it couldn't have been addressed to Christians. Verse 3 reads, "That which we have seen and heard declare we unto you, that ye also may have fellowship with us: and truly our fellowship is with the Father, and with his Son Jesus Christ." All Christians already fellowship together around Jesus Christ and other Christians.

Verse 5 reads, "This then is the message which we have heard of him, and declare unto you, that God is light, and in him is no darkness at all." Why would he have to declare to Christians that God is light?

Verse 8 says, "If we say that we have no sin, we deceive ourselves, and the truth is not in us." What Christian would ever say we have no sin? Christians already have the truth in them; that is something a Gnostic would say.

In 1 John 2:1, he called them his little children. In 1 John 2:12, he said, "I write unto you, little children, because your sins are forgiven you for his name's sake." I believe 1 John 1:9 is taken out of context. It is a major stumbling block for many Christians and so often keeps them sin-conscious rather than Jesus-conscious. Many Christians are so sin-conscious that every time a troubling circumstance arises, they think God is bringing that trouble to them because they have some unconfessed sin. I've heard from one minister whom I greatly respect that when we sin, we open the door for Satan to come in and wreak havoc in our lives. This mind-set would still cause us to be sin-conscious, which I don't think is what God wishes for His children. Remember the root of all sin is unbelief; whatever is not of faith is sin.

Unbelief causes us to focus on ourselves rather than on the goodness of God. I believe God through the Holy Spirit will bring things to our minds that we need to repent of because it will bring harm to us or others. Remember that to repent means to change your mind.

Jesus is our Savior from our sins.

CHAPTER 11

What Is the Relationship between Our Feelings, Souls, Hearts, and Emotions?

What determines our destiny—our hearts, souls, emotions, bodies, spirits, or all of them working together? What is our part, and what is God's part?

Remember we are spirits and possess souls (minds, wills, and emotions); we have hearts, and all of these are housed in our bodies. When we are born again, God does not take us out of the world; He has given us everything we need to be victorious in the world. He has given us His Holy Spirit and His Word to show to us what He has given us. Day by day, we find out what our inheritance is and work it out in our lives.

> Beloved, I wish above all things that thou mayest prosper
> and be in health, even as thy soul prospereth. (3 John 2:2)

God wants us to prosper in every area of our lives even as our soul prospers. He wants us to be healthy in our bodies and be blessed with all our physical needs met. God wants us to continuously experience His peace in our hearts and minds. He wants us to have great marriages and families and to reach the destinies He has called us to.

Well, we live in a fallen world that at times can be very trying at best. Why are some people so content and blessed while others are not? Is it just because people are in different circumstances and that determines their destinies? Can we choose our circumstances? Can we control what enters our minds? Can we control our emotions or are they determined by the situations we find ourselves in? If a thought comes to our minds, can we determine if it stays or goes away? I think the answer to all these questions is yes and no. We can't control every circumstance that comes, but we can choose by the grace of God the right responses.

By the grace of God we can choose the fruit of the spirit love, joy, peace, patience, kindness, gentleness, meekness, faith, and self-control. Let's not choose the works of the flesh.

Galatians 5:19-20

Be Slow to Anger

Proverbs 16:32 reads, "He who is slow to anger is better than the mighty, he who rules his spirit than he who takes a city." Another version reads, "It is better to be slow-tempered than famous; it is better to have self-control than to control an army."

One of the fruits of the spirit is temperance; we can exercise self-control in every area of our lives. It could be to have self-control over eating, drinking, smoking, swearing, spending money, having relationships with all types of people, and so on. What determines the amount of restraint or self-control we show in our lives? Emotions are a gift from God we are to enjoy, but sometimes, our emotions caused by negative thoughts can lead us to harmful and even destructive places. How many people end up in prison because they could not control their emotions?

We all go through trials in life. Sometimes, we go through great trials because we made the wrong choices or responded with negative emotions. How I respond in any circumstance emotionally will determine my destiny. Proverbs 16 reveals to us that those who are slow to anger are better than the mighty, that those with self-control are better than those who control armies.

Much of the battle in life is in our minds, the seat of our emotions. Emotions are painful or pleasurable feelings that can move us in the right or wrong direction. Christians must learn to master their emotions or they will master them. The weakest people are those who can't control their emotions.

The first step to controlling our emotions is reading God's Word daily. I would rather do without breakfast than neglect reading the Word. When our hearts are established with the Word, we will have the Word and fruit of the Spirit flowing out of our hearts as living water. The answer to controlling your emotions is not constant sin consciousness. It is a heart established and founded in the Word of God.

The Promise of the Holy Spirit

> On the last day, that great *day* of the feast, Jesus stood and cried out, saying, "If anyone thirsts, let him come to Me and drink. He who believes in Me, as the Scripture has said, out of his belly (heart) will flow rivers of living water." But this He spoke concerning the Spirit, whom those believing in Him would receive; for the Holy Spirit was not yet *given,* because Jesus was not yet glorified. (John 7:37–39)

> But the fruit of the Spirit is love, joy, peace, patience, kindness, goodness, faithfulness, gentleness, self-control. Against such there is no law. And those *who are* Christ's have crucified the flesh with its passions and desires. If we live in the Spirit, let us also walk in the Spirit. (Galatians 5:22–25)

When you have rivers of living water flowing out of your heart, you will find it much easier to control your thoughts and emotions. It will be easy for you to distinguish between God's thoughts and the devil's thoughts. If a thought comes to your mind, you must learn to recognize its source.

We Do Not Wrestle against Flesh and Blood

> 3 For though we walk in the flesh, we do not war after the flesh. 4 For the weapons of our warfare *are* not carnal but mighty in God for pulling down strongholds, 5 casting down (imaginations) arguments and every high thing that exalts itself against the knowledge of God, bringing every thought into captivity every thought to the obedience of Christ. (2 Corinthians 10:3-5)

Some of us have developed strongholds, fortresses we have built up in our minds over the years. These fortresses react to certain stimuli—such as words that set us off. We must learn by the Word and the power God has given to us to pull down these strongholds. We must cast down every argument or imagination that exalts itself against the knowledge of God and bring our thoughts captive to the obedience of Christ. The devil comes to steal, kill, and destroy. The only power the devil has is deception.

If we are being accused, it is not God doing that. God will lead us out of our harmful ways, but He does not condemn us. God leads, but it is up to us to follow Him. He is our Savior, our Redeemer, not our accuser. Every child of God is led by the Holy Spirit, but every child of God does not necessarily follow the leading of the Holy Spirit. Romans 8:14

Be Strong in the Lord and in the Power of His Might

A war is taking place in the world. Though we are in the flesh, we do not war in the flesh. We must recognize our enemy and his strategy. We also have to know what weapons to use against our enemy. As Christians, people are not our enemies.

> Finally, my brethren, be strong in the Lord and in the power of His might. Put on the whole armor of God, that you may be able to stand against the wiles of the devil. For we do not wrestle against flesh and blood, but against principalities, against powers, against the rulers of the darkness of this age, against spiritual *hosts* of wickedness in the heavenly *places*. Therefore take up the whole armor of God, that you may be able to withstand in the evil day, and having done all, to stand. Stand therefore, having girded your waist with truth, having put on the breastplate of righteousness, and having shod your feet with the preparation of the gospel of peace; above all, taking the shield of faith with which you will be able to quench all the fiery darts of the wicked one. And take the helmet of salvation, and the sword of the Spirit, which is the word of God; praying always with all prayer and supplication in the Spirit, being watchful to this end with all perseverance and supplication for all the saints. (Ephesians 6:10–18)

Things We Must Understand

- We are to be strong in the Lord and the power of his might, not ours.
- We must put on the whole armor of God.

- We are to stand against the wiles, schemes, and lies of the devil.
- We wrestle not against flesh and blood.
- We will have bad days, but most of our days should be good.
- We must know the truth—His Word.
- We must understand that our righteousness comes from faith in Jesus Christ.
- We must share the gospel of peace.
- We must surround ourselves with the shield of faith.
- We must grow in knowledge of the great salvation God has given us.
- We must use the Word of God as a sword against Satan as Jesus did.
- We must pray daily with all prayer and supplication in the Spirit.
- We must persevere.

Things to Remember to Help Us Reach Our Destinies

- Control your emotions or they may take you in the wrong direction.
- God has called us to be masters in life, not to be mastered by life.
- The weakest people are those who can't control their emotions.
- As your soul goes, so does your heart and life.
- If you don't master your thoughts, your bad thoughts will contaminate your heart and then your heart will pollute your soul.
- Choose your friends wisely; they will influence your destiny.
- Those who can't control their thoughts can't control their spending.
- If you don't control your emotions, you will create bad habits.
- Don't allow circumstances to govern your emotions.
- Godly thoughts and emotions produce a godly character.
- Take control of your negative emotions by immediately speaking the Word of God. As soon as you do, your thoughts will change.

- The greatest people are those with godly temperaments.
- Don't make big, quick decisions on emotions.
- Remember that your dominant emotions will determine your destiny.
- Don't blame circumstances and people for your negative emotions.
- By the grace and power of God, we can master our emotions.
- How we respond to adversity will determine our destiny.
- Don't let negative emotions determine your actions.
- Develop godly habits and a godly character; they will get you to God's destination.
- Remember Isaiah 26:3; God will keep us in perfect peace when our minds are on Him.
- No matter what the circumstances are, we have a choice to keep our minds on Him.

CHAPTER 12
God Loves Us with an Unconditional, Everlasting Love

We are blessed not because we are good but because God is good. Christians living lives of sin could face grave consequences, but they are still be the righteousness of God in Christ Jesus.

Christians doing wrong are not made unrighteous before God because it was not their good deeds or good works before they became a Christian that made them the righteousness of God.

Many times, they live sinful lives because they think they are condemned and give up thinking God can't forgive their sins. Many Christians, ignorant that grace is God's unearned, undeserved, and unmerited favor, keep thinking their good deeds or lifestyle makes and keeps them righteous before God. Nothing could be further from the truth.

God is displeased with self-righteous people, but is pleased with those who receive the abundance of grace and the gift of righteousness from Him. Our lifestyles affect the condition of our hearts and in turn, the condition of our hearts affect how we perceive God. God loves us with an unconditional, everlasting love. Christ died for us sinners. Our part is to keep on believing in Him and doing everything we can to keep doubt and unbelief out of our hearts. Remember an evil heart of unbelief hinders us from receiving all of God's grace for us. Romans 8:32 says, "He that spared not His own Son, but gave Him up for us all, how will He not freely give us all things?" God does not cease giving me things even when I sin. Let's just keep focusing on Jesus, believing, and receiving all things God has freely given us.

We don't access this grace by our good deeds but by faith free of doubt and unbelief. One of my greatest goals in life is to keep faith in my heart and mind free of doubt and unbelief. I'm responsible for keeping unbelief out of my heart because unbelief or the cares of this world, the deceitfulness of riches, and the lust for other things entering my heart choke the Word and it becomes unfruitful.

Under the old covenant, the people were constantly sin-conscious because their sacrifices could never take away sins.

> For Christ is not entered into the holy places made with hands, which are the figures of the true; but into heaven itself, now to appear in the presence of God for us: Nor yet that he should offer himself often, as the high priest entereth into the holy place every year with blood of others; For then must he often have suffered since the foundation of the world: but now once in the end of the world hath he appeared to put away sin by the sacrifice of himself. (Hebrews 9:24–26)

So many Christian are still living as if they were under the Old Testament Law by going through rituals to be cleansed of unrighteousness. Once we receive Jesus as our Lord and Savior, we are perfected forever (Hebrews 10:10–14). Sin is no longer the issue with God, so we should no longer be continually sin conscience. (Hebrews 10:2) Jesus purged our consciences of dead works to serve the living God (Hebrews 9:12–14). I believe the more sin-conscious Christians are, the more they sin. I believe the more Jesus conscious Christians are, the less they sin.

Readers who meditate on Hebrews 9–12 will find these truths: God is merciful to our unrighteousness, and our sins and iniquities He remembers no more. We have eternal redemption. Christ offered to bear the sins of many; He took away the first to establish the second in which there is no more consciousness of sins. Through His body, we are sanctified once and for all. He has by one offering perfected forever them that are sanctified. Our hearts have been cleansed of evil consciences, and putting the Word in our hearts daily keeps it in the right condition. There is no more offering for sin because Jesus has remitted it.

If every time we sin, we lose our righteousness, then it's only by doing good that we keep our righteousness. If that is the case, then it must be our good works in the first place that made us righteous. This is not what the scriptures teach us. Our righteousness comes by faith in Jesus Christ alone, not by any of our good works.

> Knowing that a man is not justified by the works of the law, but by the faith of Jesus Christ, even we have believed in Jesus Christ, that we might be justified by the faith of Christ, and not by the works of the law: for by the works of the law shall no flesh be justified. (Galatians 2:16)

> For I will be merciful to their unrighteousness, and their sins and their iniquities will I remember no more. (Hebrews 8:12 and 10:16–18)

More New Testament Scriptures on the Heart

Study these forty-nine scriptures in context with the verses before and after them and the rest of the Bible.

- Acts 11:23: Who, when he came, and had seen the grace of God, was glad, and exhorted them all, that with purpose of heart they would cleave unto the Lord.

- Acts 13:22: And when he had removed him, he raised up unto them David to be their king; to whom also he gave their testimony, and said, I have found David the son of Jesse, a man after mine own heart, which shall fulfil all my will.
- Acts 15:8: And God, which knoweth the hearts, bare them witness, giving them the Holy Ghost, even as he did unto us.
- Acts 15:9: And put no difference between us and them, purifying their hearts by faith.
- Romans 1:21: Because that, when they knew God, they glorified him not as God, neither were thankful; but became vain in their imaginations, and their foolish heart was darkened.
- Romans 1:24: Wherefore God also gave them up to uncleanness through the lusts of their own hearts, to dishonour their own bodies between themselves.
- Romans 2:5: But after thy hardness and impenitent heart treasurest up unto thyself wrath against the day of wrath and revelation of the righteous judgment of God.
- Romans 5:5: And hope maketh not ashamed; because the love of God is shed abroad in our hearts by the Holy Ghost which is given unto us.
- Romans 6:17: But God be thanked, that ye were the servants of sin, but ye have obeyed from the heart that form of doctrine which was delivered you.
- Romans 8:27: And he that searcheth the hearts knoweth what is the mind of the Spirit, because he maketh intercession for the saints according to the will of God.
- Romans 10:8: But what saith it? The word is nigh thee, even in thy mouth, and in thy heart: that is, the word of faith, which we preach.
- Romans 10:9: That if thou shalt confess with thy mouth the Lord Jesus, and shalt believe in thine heart that God hath raised him from the dead, thou shalt be saved.

- Romans 10:10: For with the heart man believeth unto righteousness; and with the mouth confession is made unto salvation.
- Romans 16:18: For they that are such serve not our Lord Jesus Christ, but their own belly; and by good words and fair speeches deceive the hearts of the simple.
- 1 Corinthians 2:9: But as it is written, Eye hath not seen, nor ear heard, neither have entered into the heart of man, the things which God hath prepared for them that love him.
- 1 Corinthians 4:5: Therefore judge nothing before the time, until the Lord come, who both will bring to light the hidden things of darkness, and will make manifest the counsels of the hearts: and then shall every man have praise of God.
- 1 Corinthians 7:37: Nevertheless he that standeth stedfast in his heart, having no necessity, but hath power over his own will, and hath so decreed in his heart that he will keep his virgin, doeth well.
- 1 Corinthians 14:25: And thus are the secrets of his heart made manifest; and so falling down on his face he will worship God, and report that God is in you of a truth.
- 2 Corinthians 1:22: Who hath also sealed us, and given the earnest of the Spirit in our hearts.
- 2 Corinthians 4:6: For God, who commanded the light to shine out of darkness, hath shined in our hearts, to give the light of the knowledge of the glory of God in the face of Jesus Christ.
- 2 Corinthians 9:7: Every man according as he purposeth in his heart, so let him give; not grudgingly, or of necessity: for God loveth a cheerful giver.
- Galatians 4:6: And because ye are sons, God hath sent forth the Spirit of his Son into your hearts, crying, Abba, Father.
- Ephesians 3:17: That Christ may dwell in your hearts by faith; that ye, being rooted and grounded in love.

- Ephesians 4:18: Having the understanding darkened, being alienated from the life of God through the ignorance that is in them, because of the blindness of their heart.

- Ephesians 5:19: Speaking to yourselves in psalms and hymns and spiritual songs, singing and making melody in your heart to the Lord.

- Philippians 4:7: And the peace of God, which passeth all understanding, shall keep your hearts and minds through Christ Jesus.

- Colossians 3:15: And let the peace of God rule in your hearts, to the which also ye are called in one body; and be ye thankful.

- Colossians 3:16: Let the word of Christ dwell in you richly in all wisdom; teaching and admonishing one another in psalms and hymns and spiritual songs, singing with grace in your hearts to the Lord.

- 1 Thessalonians 2:4: But as we were allowed of God to be put in trust with the gospel, even so we speak; not as pleasing men, but God, which trieth our hearts.

- 1 Thessalonians 3:13: To the end he may stablish your hearts unblameable in holiness before God, even our Father, at the coming of our Lord Jesus Christ with all his saints.

- 2 Thessalonians 3:5: And the Lord direct your hearts into the love of God, and into the patient waiting for Christ.

- 1 Timothy 1:5: Now the end of the commandment is charity out of a pure heart, and of a good conscience, and of faith unfeigned.

- Hebrews 3:10: Wherefore I was grieved with that generation, and said, They do alway err in their heart; and they have not known my ways.

- Hebrews 3:12: Take heed, brethren, lest there be in any of you an evil heart of unbelief, in departing from the living God. Christians can have an evil heart of unbelief.

- Hebrews 4:12: For the word of God is quick, and powerful, and sharper than any twoedged sword, piercing even to the dividing asunder of soul and spirit, and of the joints and marrow, and is a discerner of the thoughts and intents of the heart.
- Hebrews 10:22: Let us draw near with a true heart in full assurance of faith, having our hearts sprinkled from an evil conscience, and our bodies washed with pure water.
- Hebrews 13:9: Be not carried about with divers and strange doctrines. For it is a good thing that the heart be established with grace; not with meats, which have not profited them that have been occupied therein.
- James 1:26: If any man among you seem to be religious, and bridleth not his tongue, but deceiveth his own heart, this man's religion is vain.
- James 3:14: But if ye have bitter envying and strife in your hearts, glory not, and lie not against the truth.
- James 4:8: Draw nigh to God, and he will draw nigh to you. Cleanse your hands, ye sinners; and purify your hearts, ye double minded.
- 1 Peter 1:22: Seeing ye have purified your souls in obeying the truth through the Spirit unto unfeigned love of the brethren, see that ye love one another with a pure heart fervently.
- 1 Peter 3:4: But let it be [the inner beauty of] the hidden person of the heart, with the imperishable quality *and* unfading charm of a gentle and peaceful spirit, [one that is calm and self-controlled, not overanxious, but serene and spiritually mature] which is very precious in the sight of God.
- 1 Peter 3:15: But sanctify the Lord God in your hearts: and be ready always to give an answer to every man that asketh you a reason of the hope that is in you with meekness and fear.

- 2 Peter 2:14: Having eyes full of adultery, and that cannot cease from sin; beguiling unstable souls: an heart they have exercised (trained) with covetous practices; cursed children: Read whole chapter.
- 1 John 3:19: And hereby we know that we are of the truth, and shall assure our hearts before him.
- 1 John 3:21: Beloved, if our heart condemn us not, then have we confidence toward God.
- Revelation 2:23: And I will kill her children with death; and all the churches shall know that I am he which searcheth the reins and hearts: and I will give unto every one of you according to your works.
- Revelation 18:7: How much she hath glorified herself, and lived deliciously, so much torment and sorrow give her: for she saith in her heart, I sit a queen, and am no widow, and shall see no sorrow.

CHAPTER 13

Is Your Heart Saturated with Secular Humanism?

I was a public high school science teacher for twenty-one years. I taught AP biology, chemistry, earth science, physical science, anatomy, and physiology. I know a little bit about what I write here. Many things in the science curriculum, that if taken as fact, will create in your heart a lot of unbelief and hardness. Most of us today have what I call a secular humanistic education, which really shows up in the fields of science, history, and law. As Christians, we should have a totally biblical worldview, but most of us don't.

In the last eighty-five or so years, science started developing a materialistic worldview. This was not always the case. Most of the early scientists were biblical creationists such as Sir Isaac Newton, Carolus Linnaeus, Louis Pasteur, Gregor Mendel, and many more. Today, scientists believe that everything came about in nature by time and chance without any intelligent design, and that is what is being taught in secular science classes. Their philosophy is that nothing in nature has come into existence through purpose and design. Science is trying to explain how everything came into being without God. If you have a high school degree or a degree from any one of 90 percent of the universities in the world, your heart has been trained in the philosophy of secular humanism in abundance but you probably don't even realize it. Let me explain.

Operational science and origin science are the two types of science. For me, only operational science is true science; it is based on the present, and it is the study of present systems that can be directly observed, tested, repeated, experimentally verified, and falsified. Operational science produces all the technology we use today—computers, rockets, cars, MRIs, cell phones, nuclear bombs—the list goes on and on. These were the result of millions of hours of testable and repeatable knowledge.

Origin science tries to explain how the natural world came about without any intelligence by time and chance. This is nothing more than telling unverifiable stories that happened long, long ago and far, far away. Every method Christian or secular scientists use to date the earth start with assumptions that we are seldom presented with when dates are given. These long, long ago and far, far away stories, make for good bedtime stories, but not good science. Scientists cannot repeat any past unobserved, singular event.

We are constantly told in our textbooks how the theory of evolution is a fact by scientists who start with assumptions—the theory of evolution—and call it science. Christian students constantly hear these stories. Those who have not learned the problems with these ideas will have hearts cold and hardened to the Word of God and will probably have little interest in going to church or in God's Word.

Do the Laws of Science Support the Theory of Evolution?

Not at all. Let me explain. The law of entropy basically says that in a closed system, usable energy always decreases as time goes on. They have found it works the same in an open system as well. Another way to explain the law of entropy is that in any system, the order or complexity in the system tends to decrease as time goes on unless you have controlled energy or designed information acting on that system that is preventing degeneration.

Basically, what we observe in the natural world is that anything left on its own is degenerating. This is called the law of disorder; it goes from order to disorder. No matter how well we live and take care of ourselves, scientist observe that the human genome as a whole is degenerating at a rate of 1 to 2 percent per generation. The Bible told us this was happening thousands of years ago. It says that the earth is growing old like a garment, that the earth is passing away and is subject to corruption.

Some other laws that contradict the theory of evolution are the laws of disorder, the law of cause and effect, and the laws of chemistry, biogenesis, and physics. If scientists were honest, they would have to admit there has to be a creator or designer, but their philosophy will not allow that explanation. Any scientist who works for a secular university and starts teaching all the problems with the theory of evolution would be taking a chance on losing his or her position, grants, and tenure and being ostracized by peers. It is not to the benefit for any secular scientist to criticize Charles Darwin.

I have spent thousands of hours looking at creation vs. the theory of evolution and challenge any scientist who believes that the theory of evolution is a good explanation for how everything came about in nature to debate me.

CHAPTER 14

Could the "All Things" in Romans 8:28 Be "All Things" God Has Given Us and Not "All Things" That Happen to Us?

> Likewise the Spirit also helps our infirmities: for we know not what we should pray for as we ought: but the Spirit itself makes intercession for us with groanings which cannot be uttered. And he that searches the hearts knows what is the mind of the Spirit, because he makes intercession for the saints according to the will of God. And we know that all things work together for good to them that love God, to them who are the called according to his purpose. For whom he did foreknow, he also did predestinate to be conformed to the image of his Son, that he might be the firstborn among many brethren. (Romans 8:26–29)

Romans 8:28 is one of the most quoted scriptures of the Bible. Usually, it is quoted when someone is going through a trial or difficult time. It seems most people, even including some ministers who have greatly influenced my life for the good, believe that this verse means all things that happen to us work together for good. Of course God can work for good in all things that happen to us, but what is the true interpretation of this verse? Even if what we believe is sometimes true about the scripture, that does not mean we have the correct interpretation. The wrong interpretation of scripture will produce unbelief in our hearts.

> Knowing this first, that no prophecy of the scripture is
> of any private interpretation. (2 Peter 1:20)

Please pray and read what I have to say about Romans 8:28 and all the scriptures I use to support what I believe is the correct interpretation.

For most of my Christian life, I have wondered why most people interpret Romans 8:28 as the Living Bible does above. Verse 28 reads, "And we know that all that happens to us is working for our good if we love God and are fitting into his plans." If the apostle Paul was referring to some experience he had gone through in the proceeding verses, I could see how a person would interpret Romans 8:28 as things that happen to us.

I have read over fifty-five versions of Romans 8:28, and most of them use the wording, "We know all things work together for good to them who love God and are called according to His purpose." Why do most Christian assume the "all things" are things that happen to us? "All things" or "all the things" or "all those things" or "all these things" are used over two hundred times in the New Testament. "All things" is used to express a number of different subjects. For example, "all things whatsoever ye would that men should do," "All things are delivered unto me of my Father," "gather out of his kingdom all things," "with God all things are possible, "Teaching them to observe all things," "told him all things both what they had done," "He hath done all things well," "had given all things into his hands," "all things that I have heard," "knowing all things that should come upon him," "knowing that all things were now accomplished," "until the times of restitution of all things," "we do all things dearly beloved for your edifying," "all things are become new," "all things are for your sakes that the abundant grace," "in all these things we are more than conquerors," "for the Spirit searches all things"—there are over a hundred more.

Every one of these 229 verses in the New Testament containing "all things" and its variants must be interpreted in context or you may get a totally wrong meaning. Any one scripture must be interpreted by all the scriptures. We must also look at the verses before and after the verse for it to be interpreted correctly. Is there another scripture in the New Testament that leads us to believe God works for good in all things that happen to those who love Him and are called according to His purpose? I have not found any I think back up that reasoning. Many scriptures tell us that through the Spirit, we learn of the things God has given us.

These Scriptures Back Up My Point

> For what man knows the things of a man, save the spirit of man which is in him? even so the things of God knows no man, but the Spirit of God. Now we have received, not the spirit of the world, but the spirit which is of God; that we might know the things that are freely given to us of God. Which things also we speak, not in the words which man's wisdom teaches, but which the Holy Ghost teaches; comparing spiritual things with spiritual. But the natural man receives not the things of the Spirit of God: for they are foolishness unto him: neither can he know them, because they are spiritually discerned. (1 Corinthians 2:11–14)

To me, 1 Corinthians 1–3 speaks about the things that God has given us and the things He has prepared for us. Read chapters 1–3 and specifically 2:9–13. Verse 12 is so plain; how can we miss it? God has given His Spirit so we might know what He has given us. One main purpose of the Holy Spirit is for us to know what God has given us. Remember that the spiritual world created the natural world. It is eternal while the natural is temporal. Let's go through chapters 1–3 and look at what God wants us to grasp.

> Now we have received, not the spirit of the world, but the
> spirit which is of God; that we might know the things that
> are freely given to us of God. Which things also we speak,
> not in the words which man's wisdom teaches, but which
> the Holy Ghost teaches; comparing spiritual things with
> spiritual. (1 Corinthians 2:12–13)

For the most part, Paul was focused on spiritual things given us that are understood only by the Spirit. Here are some of the spiritual things listed in chapters 1–3. In 1:30, we are in Christ Jesus, who made unto us wisdom, righteousness, sanctification, and redemption. These are gifts we receive so we can glory in the Lord. We read in 2:4 that we can operate as Paul in demonstration of the Spirit and power. In verse 2:9, we read God has prepared for those who love Him something awesome that eye hath not seen, nor ear heard, nor heart received. In verses 3:8–9, we read every person shall receive his reward according to his labor, but we are all laborers with God. We labor in vain if we do not know what these gifts are and do not receive them. If our hearts are full of the world and not God's Word, I doubt many of these gifts will be operating in us.

Remember it was His pleasure to give us this kingdom. Let's find it and take it.

> Likewise the Spirit also helps our infirmities: for we
> know not what we should pray for as we ought: but the
> Spirit itself makes intercession for us with groanings
> which cannot be uttered. And he that searches the hearts
> knows what is the mind of the Spirit, because he makes

intercession for the saints according to the will of God. And we know that all things work together for good to them that love God, to them who are the called according to his purpose. For whom he did foreknow, he also did predestinate to be conformed to the image of his Son, that he might be the firstborn among many brethren. Moreover whom he did predestinate, them he also called: and whom he called, them he also justified: and whom he justified, them he also glorified. What shall we then say to these things? If God be for us, who can be against us? He that spared not his own Son, but delivered him up for us all, how shall he not with him also freely give us all things? (Romans 8:26–32)

Grace and peace be multiplied unto you through the knowledge of God, and of Jesus our Lord, According as **his divine power hath given unto us all things that pertain unto life and godliness**, through the knowledge of him that hath called us to glory and virtue: **Whereby are given unto us exceeding great and precious promises:** that by these ye might be partakers of the divine nature, having escaped the corruption that is in the world through lust. (2 Peter 1:2–4)

This is how I would explain the way Paul meant us to understand it: "And we know that all things that God has given to us—this great and wonderful salvation through Jesus Christ our Lord—is working for our victory in every situation we are in and all our sufferings and tribulations that we encounter in life."

I might pray a prayer of thanksgiving like this to back up how I would interpret Romans 8:28.

Father, I thank You that You have given me the Holy Spirit so I can know the things You have freely given me. Father, I thank You that the Holy Spirit helps my infirmities, intercedes for me, and has predestined me to be conformed to the image of Your Son through the Word of God. Thank you, Father, that through Your divine power, You have freely given me all things that pertain to life and godliness through the knowledge of God and gave me exceedingly great and precious promises. Yes, Father, all the things You have given me are working for my good because You love me so I could love You and be called according to Your purpose.

All through the book of Romans and especially Romans 8, Paul referred to what God has given or done for us. Here is a list of things that God has done or given to us in Romans 8 that work together for our good. Number 14, which is Romans 8:32, says it all.

1. No condemnation to them which are in Christ Jesus.
2. Law of the Spirit of life in Christ Jesus hath made me free from the law of sin and death.
3. The righteousness of the law might be fulfilled in us.
4. The Spirit is life because of righteousness.
5. Ye have received the Spirit of adoption.
6. We are the children of God.
7. Heirs of God and joint heirs with Christ.
8. The Spirit also helps our infirmities.
9. He makes intercession for the saints according to the will of God.
10. He also did predestinate us to be conformed to the image of his Son.
11. That he might be the firstborn among many brethren.
12. Whom he did predestinate, them he also called: and whom he called, them he also justified: and whom he justified, them he also glorified.
13. If God be for us, who can be against us?
14. **He that spared not his own Son, but delivered him up for us all, how shall he not with him also freely give us all things?**

(all these things He has given to us are working together for our good)

15. It is God who justifies.
16. Who also makes intercession for us.

> Who shall separate us from the love of Christ? shall tribulation, or distress, or persecution, or famine, or nakedness, or peril, or sword? As it is written, For thy sake we are killed all the day long; we are accounted as sheep for the slaughter. Nay, in all these things we are more than conquerors through him that loved us. (Romans 8:35–37)

It is not the things that happen to us that work together for our good but the things He has given us that work together for our good to make us more than conquerors through every tribulation that comes to us.

Below are other scriptures I believe verify my interpretation of Romans 8:28.

- 1 Corinthians 2:12: Now we have received, not the spirit of the world, but the spirit which is of God; that we might know the things that are freely given to us of God.
- 2 Corinthians 4:15: For all things are for your sakes, that the abundant grace might through the thanksgiving of many redound to the glory of God.
- 2 Corinthians 5:17–21: Therefore if any man be in Christ, he is a new creature: old things are passed away; behold, all things are become new. And all things are of God, who hath reconciled us to himself by Jesus Christ, and hath given to us the ministry of reconciliation; To wit, that God was in Christ, reconciling the world unto himself, not imputing their trespasses unto them; and hath committed unto us the word of reconciliation. Now then we are ambassadors for Christ, as though God did beseech you by

us: we pray you in Christ's stead, be ye reconciled to God. For he hath made him to be sin for us, who knew no sin; that we might be made the righteousness of God in him.

- 2 Peter 1:2–4: Grace and peace be multiplied unto you through the knowledge of God, and of Jesus our Lord, According as his divine power hath given unto us all things that pertain unto life and godliness, through the knowledge of him that hath called us to glory and virtue: Whereby are given unto us exceeding great and precious promises: that by these ye might be partakers of the divine nature, having escaped the corruption that is in the world through lust.

- Romans 8:32: He that spared not his own Son, but delivered him up for us all, **how shall he not with him also freely give us all things.**

I am not writing this book to gain popularity. I understand that Romans 8:28 has been used to comfort Christians, who love God and are called according to His purpose; in all the bad things that happen to them. I know God is able to take the things that Satan has brought about to destroy us and can turn it around for our good. We must remember that God has given us authority over all the powers of the enemy. We are told to resist the devil and he will flee from us. Satan is constantly working against us to steal, kill and destroy. If we honestly believe that everything that happens to us will work out for our good, then why would we resist anything? This kind of attitude makes us very passive and puts all the responsibility on God. We are always given the choice by God in everything that happens to us, to respond in faith, with the great salvation that He has given to us, to overcome this world. If we allow Satan to bring into our lives all kinds of evil things, God has to allow it because we allowed it. Jesus said whatsoever we bind on earth shall be bound in heaven and whatsoever we loose on earth shall be loosed in heaven.

Matthew 16:19

And I will give unto thee the keys of the kingdom of heaven: and whatsoever thou shalt bind on earth shall be bound in heaven: and whatsoever thou shalt loose on earth shall be loosed in heaven.

CHAPTER 15

Why Did Jesus Say, "You Must Be Born Again"?

Let's start from the beginning, Genesis 1–3. If we don't understand what happened at the beginning, nothing else makes much sense. This is a short summary of Genesis 1–3.

In the beginning, God created the heavens and the earth. After He finished His creation in six literal days, He rested from all His work, and He saw everything He had made and beheld it was very good. (This original very good earth became subject to corruption after the fall of man, and perished 1600 years later in the flood of Noah; see Romans 8:20-23 and 2 Peter 3:6 KJV) The earth had perfect weather and no disease, birth defects, tornados, earthquakes, floods, hurricanes, death, or wars.

Man was created in God's image and likeness and was given dominion and authority over all creation. God told man to be fruitful and multiply and fill all the earth.

God loved Adam and Eve. He communed with them in the cool of the day. He placed the man and the woman in the Garden of Eden to dress it and keep it. God told man he could eat from every tree of the garden except for the Tree of Knowledge of Good and Evil. If he ate from that tree, he would die (in dying, you will begin to die).

Long Story Short

Satan tempted Adam and Eve to eat the fruit from that tree, and all creation became cursed. When the fall came to God's original very good creation because of man's sin, man's heart became incurably sick, his right relationship with God died, and his body began to die even though he lived 930 years.

> The heart is deceitful above all things, and desperately wicked (incurably sick): who can know it? (Jeremiah 17:9)

Mankind, all plants, animals, and the ground were cursed because of man's disobedience. Satan took authority over earth and became the god of this world (2 Corinthians 4:4; Luke 4:5–8). Of course, God still loved mankind and did all He could to bring man back into a right relationship with Himself. God would look for people who would obey Him so He could bring salvation into their lives. He could work only through people who believed in what He said to them, for instance, Abraham. The Bible says that Abraham believed God and it was counted to him for righteousness. But the result of man's disobedience devastated all creation.

> For the creature was made subject to vanity, not willingly, but by reason of him who hath subjected the same in hope. Because the creature itself also shall be delivered from the bondage of corruption and decay into the glorious liberty of the children of God. (Romans 8:20–21)

> And the Lord God said unto the serpent, Because thou hast done this, thou art cursed above all cattle, and above every beast of the field; upon thy belly shalt thou go, and dust shalt thou eat all the days of thy life: And I will put enmity between thee and the woman, and between thy

seed and her seed; it shall bruise thy head (Jesus would accomplish this when He would become a man), and thou shalt bruise his heel. Unto the woman he said, I will greatly multiply thy sorrow and thy conception; in sorrow thou shalt bring forth children; and thy desire shall be to thy husband, and he shall rule over thee. And unto Adam he said, Because thou hast hearkened unto the voice of thy wife, and hast eaten of the tree, of which I commanded thee, saying, Thou shalt not eat of it: cursed is the ground for thy sake; in sorrow shalt thou eat of it all the days of thy life; Thorns also and thistles shall it bring forth to thee; and thou shalt eat the herb of the field; In the sweat of thy face shalt thou eat bread, till thou return unto the ground; for out of it wast thou taken: for dust thou art, and unto dust shalt thou return. (Genesis 3:14–19)

Noah's Flood

Some scriptures give ideas about what happened during the flood. I believe this historic event of the earth is very important for us to understand so we can better understand how different the earth is today from what it was before the flood. Many Christians today look at the earth as if it were the way God originally created it with a few bad spots here and there. This misconception of God's creation might give us the wrong understanding of God's nature and characteristics. Thousands of the original plants and animals have become extinct because the environment today is much harsher than that of the original created earth.

If God had not destroyed all but eight human beings, man would have destroyed all hope of God redeeming mankind. The Bible says,

5 And God saw that the wickedness of man was great in the earth, and that every imagination of the thoughts of his heart was only evil continually.

6 And it repented the Lord that he had made man on the earth, and it grieved him at his heart.

7 And the Lord said, I will destroy man whom I have created from the face of the earth; both man, and beast, and the creeping thing, and the fowls of the air; for it repents me that I have made them.

8 But Noah found grace in the eyes of the Lord.

12 And God looked upon the earth, and, behold, it was corrupt; for all flesh had corrupted his way upon the earth.

13 And God said unto Noah, The end of all flesh is come before me; for the earth is filled with violence through them; and, behold, I will destroy them with the earth.

11 In the six hundredth year of Noah's life, in the second month, the seventeenth day of the month, the same day were all the fountains of the great deep broken up, (another translation says fountains all burst forth) and the windows of heaven were opened.

12 And the rain was upon the earth forty days and forty nights. (Genesis 6:5–8)

Many creation scientists believed that the bursting of the fountains of the great deep would have produced a huge amount of superheated water bursting high into the atmosphere and even into outer space producing comets. Mainstream scientists don't have a good explanation for the comets.

The best explanation of the thousands of miles of fault lines that run around the earth is the worldwide flood of Noah's day.

For more information on the HPT, check out Dr. Walt Brown's http://creationscience.com and Real Science Radio's http://rsr.org/hydroplate-theory resource page.

Peter Gave Us a Good Explanation of the Pre-Flood, Present, and Future Earth Conditions

> For this they willingly are ignorant of, that by the word of God the heavens were of old, and the earth standing out of the water and in the water: Whereby the world that then was, being overflowed with water, perished: But the heavens and the earth, which are now, by the same word are kept in store, reserved unto fire against the day of judgment and perdition of ungodly men. But, beloved, be not ignorant of this one thing, that one day is with the Lord as a thousand years, and a thousand years as one day. The Lord is not slack concerning his promise, as some men count slackness; but is longsuffering to us-ward, not willing that any should perish, but that all should come to repentance. But the day of the Lord will come as a thief in the night; in the which the heavens shall pass away with a great noise, and the elements shall melt with fervent heat, the earth also and the works that are therein shall be burned up. Seeing then that all these things shall be dissolved, what manner of persons ought ye to be in all holy conversation and godliness, Looking for and

hasting unto the coming of the day of God, wherein the heavens being on fire shall be dissolved, and the elements shall melt with fervent heat? Nevertheless we, according to his promise, look for new heavens and a new earth, wherein dwelleth righteousness. (2 Peter 3:5–13)

My hope is not in this cursed physical creation that is passing away (2 John 2:17). The original earth was first cursed and then perished during the flood. This earth is reserved unto fire and shall be burned up and dissolved. The earth's elements will melt from fervent heat. It is not something God considers worth saving.

I realize there is beauty in many places, but it is not near as beautiful as God's original very good creation. It is hard for us to see it because we never saw the original earth. We were not there when the earth was filled with peaceful dinosaurs, lions, and serpents that would not hurt man and ate only plants. If you drive across the United States, you will see many spectacular geologic formations left from the catastrophic flood. Almost all the rock formations across the globe were laid down during the flood. Mainstream scientists want you to believe it took 500 million years to lay these layers down by slow and gradual processes.

The best explanation is that these layers were laid down rapidly as the earth was turned inside out and upside down during the flood. Fossils in rock layers could have been preserved only if they had been covered up very rapidly by fast-moving water filled with all kinds and sizes of sedimentary particles that turned to hard rock, as concrete does. As these superheated fountains of the great deep broke up and burst forth, an unimaginable amount of erosion of earth's bedrock took place. For 150 days, the waters increased and eroded the earth's foundation and then deposited rocks in layers all around earth.

The flood was devastating to the earth's surface. That is why we see billions of dead things, in rock layers, laid down by water all over the earth.

After and while these layers were being laid down, many mountains were being raised to the levels they are today. That is why we find fossils at the top of many high mountains.

Some Theologians Have Compromised the Word of God because of Secular Science

I believe there is little or no basis in scripture or in scientific evidence for the age of the earth to be more the six thousand years old. Mainstream science based on a materialistic philosophy has duped the Christian world into believing the earth is 4.5 billion years old.

After theologians bought into the concept of the earth being billions of years old, theologians came up with an explanation in the Bible to try to make it fit what mainstream science told them. This idea was called the gap theory popularized by Thomas Chalmers in 1814. It proposed millions or billions of years between Genesis 1:1 and 1:2. They say this is the time God cast out Satan and his angels from heaven when they rebelled against Him.

They say this is when there was a pre-Adamic race. God finally destroyed this pre-Adamic earth with a flood and restored it for man. I think it's sad that we took the word of mainstream scientists who were trying to explain how everything came about by time and chance without God. Many scriptures were ignored, and theologians came up with an explanation that they thought would fit old-earth science.

The gap theory is a bad idea because it does not support so many other scriptures such as "In the beginning of creation, God created them male and female", since time began, or when the foundations of the earth formed. The biggest problem with it is that you have death before man's sin. Adam's sin brought death into the world, but if the earth is billions of years old, with all these dead things laid down in rock layers already here before Adam was created, Adam's sin was not the cause of death on earth. But we know from the scriptures that Adam's sin brought death into the world. Romans 5:12

This scripture gives a much better explanation about where Satan came from.

> Son of man, take up a lamentation upon the king of Tyrus, and say unto him, Thus saith the Lord God; Thou sealest up the sum, full of wisdom, and perfect in beauty. Thou hast been in Eden the garden of God; every precious stone was thy covering, the sardius, topaz, and the diamond, the beryl, the onyx, and the jasper, the sapphire, the emerald, and the carbuncle, and gold: the workmanship of thy tabrets and of thy pipes was prepared in thee in the day that thou wast created. Thou art the anointed cherub (angel) that covereth; and I have set thee so: thou wast upon the holy mountain of God; thou hast walked up and down in the midst of the stones of fire. Thou wast perfect in thy ways from the day that thou wast created, till iniquity was found in thee. (Ezekiel 28:12–15)

I think Ezekiel 28 and other scriptures give a better explanation of where Satan came from. While he was in the garden, he was Lucifer, perfect in beauty; every precious stone was his covering as the anointed cherub, and he was perfect in all his ways until iniquity was found in him.

Lucifer as a ministering spirit (Hebrews 1:14) to Adam in the garden persuaded him to eat the fruit God told him not to eat. That is when Lucifer became Satan, the god of this world.

The New Testament makes little sense without the Old Testament. The scriptures in the Old Testament are types and foreshadowings of the New Testament.

Below is a list of New Testament scriptures that reveal the importance of the Old Testament scriptures

- Matthew 22:29: Jesus answered and said unto them, Ye do err, not knowing the scriptures, nor the power of God.
- Matthew 26:56: But all this was done, that the scriptures of the prophets might be fulfilled. Then all the disciples forsook him, and fled.
- Luke 24:27: And beginning at Moses and all the prophets, he expounded unto them in all the scriptures the things concerning himself.
- Luke 24:32: And they said one to another, Did not our heart burn within us, while he talked with us by the way, and while he opened to us the scriptures?
- Luke 24:45: Then opened he their understanding, that they might understand the scriptures.
- John 5:39: Search the scriptures; for in them ye think ye have eternal life: and they are they which testify of me.
- Acts 2:16–17: But this is that which was spoken by the prophet Joel; And it shall come to pass in the last days, saith God, I will pour out of my Spirit upon all flesh: and your sons and your daughters shall prophesy, and your young men shall see visions, and your old men shall dream dreams.
- Acts 17:2: And Paul, as his manner was, went in unto them, and three sabbath days reasoned with them out of the scriptures.
- Acts 17:11: These were more noble than those in Thessalonica, in that they received the word with all readiness of mind, and searched the scriptures daily, whether those things were so.
- Acts 18:28: For he mightily convinced the Jews, and that publicly, shewing by the scriptures that Jesus was Christ.

- Romans 1:2: … which he had promised afore by his prophets in the holy scriptures.

- Romans 15:4: For whatsoever things were written aforetime were written for our learning, that we through patience and comfort of the scriptures might have hope.

- Romans 16:26: But now is made manifest, and by the scriptures of the prophets, according to the commandment of the everlasting God, made known to all nations for the obedience of faith.

- 1 Corinthians 15:3: For I delivered unto you first of all that which I also received, how that Christ died for our sins according to the scriptures.

- 1 Corinthians 15:4: And that he was buried, and that he rose again the third day according to the scriptures.

- 2 Timothy 3:15: And that from a child thou hast known the holy scriptures, which are able to make thee wise unto salvation through faith which is in Christ Jesus

- The New Testament makes little sense without the Old Testament. The Scriptures in the Old Testament are types and shadows of the New Testament.

There are thousands of references to the Old Testament Scriptures in the New Testament. In the Old Testament, the New Testament is concealed, and in the New Testament the Old Testament is revealed or fulfilled.

God Appeared to Abraham about 2,000 Years after Creation

Now the Lord had said unto Abram, Get thee out of thy country, and from thy kindred, and from thy father's house, unto a land that I will show thee: And I will make of thee a great nation, and I will bless thee, and make thy name great; and thou shalt be a blessing: And I will bless them that bless thee, and curse him that curses thee: and in thee shall all families of the earth be blessed. (Genesis 12:1–3)

(Romans 4:1–25)

What shall we say then that Abraham our father, as pertaining to the flesh, hath found? For if Abraham were justified by works, he hath whereof to glory; but not before God. For what saith the scripture? Abraham believed God, and it was counted unto him for righteousness. Now to him that works is the reward not reckoned of grace, but of debt. But to him that works not, but believes on him that justifies the ungodly, his faith is counted for righteousness. Even as David also describes blessedness of the man, unto whom God imputes righteousness without works, Saying, Blessed are they whose iniquities are forgiven, and whose sins are covered. Blessed is the man to whom the Lord will not impute sin. Cometh this blessedness then upon the circumcision only, or upon the uncircumcision also? for we say that faith was reckoned to Abraham for righteousness. How was it then reckoned? when he was in circumcision, or in uncircumcision? Not in circumcision, but in uncircumcision. And he received the sign of circumcision, a seal of the righteousness of the faith which he had yet being uncircumcised: that he might be the father of all them that believe, though they be not circumcised; that righteousness might be imputed unto them also: And the father of circumcision to them who are not of the circumcision only, but who also walk in the steps of that faith of our father Abraham, which he had being yet uncircumcised. For the promise, that he should be the heir of the world, was not to Abraham, or to his seed, through the law, but through the righteousness of faith. For if they which are of the law be heirs, faith is made void, and the promise made of none effect: Because the law works wrath: for where no law is, there is no transgression. Therefore it is of faith, that it might be by grace; to the end the promise might be sure to all the seed; not to that only which is of the law, but to that also which is of the faith of Abraham; who is the father of us all, (As it is written, I have made thee a father of many nations,) before him whom he believed, even God, who quickens the dead, and calls those things which be not as though they were. Who against hope believed in hope, that he might become the father of many nations, according to that which was spoken, So shall thy seed be. And being not weak in faith, he considered not his own body now dead, when he was about an hundred years old, neither yet the deadness of Sarah's womb: He staggered not at the promise of God through unbelief; but was strong in faith, giving glory to God; And being fully persuaded that, what he had promised, he was able also to perform. And therefore it was imputed to him for righteousness. Now it was not written for his sake alone, that it was imputed to him; But for us also, to whom it shall be imputed, if we believe on him that raised up Jesus our Lord from the dead; Who was delivered for our offences, and was raised again for our justification. (Romans 4:1–25)

Abraham was not under the law but under grace, so grace came four hundred years before the law.

Abraham believed God, and it was counted unto him for righteousness.

God promised Abraham that he would be the father of many nations: "According to that which was spoken so shall thy seed be" (v. 18 above). This seed was Christ, who came from the lineage of Abraham. So God blessed Abraham not because he was good but because Abraham believed God; thus, he became the father of many nations.

Moses Gave the Children of Israel the Law

> For the law was given by Moses, but grace and truth came
> by Jesus Christ. (John 1:17)

About 2,500 years after creation, God delivered the children of Abraham, Isaac, and Jacob through Moses from the bondage of Pharaoh in Egypt. By many miracles, God led them to the wilderness of Sinai and gave them the Law of Moses. Up to that point, sin was in the world, but sin is not imputed when there is no law.

Some Scriptures on the Law from the New Testament

> What then? are we better than they? No, in no wise: for
> we have before proved both Jews and Gentiles, that they
> are all under sin; As it is written, There is none righteous,
> no, not one: There is none that understands, there is
> none that seeks after God. They are all gone out of the
> way, they are together become unprofitable; there is none
> that does good, no, not one. Their throat is an open
> sepulchre; with their tongues they have used deceit; the
> poison of asps is under their lips: Whose mouth is full of
> cursing and bitterness: Their feet are swift to shed blood:
> Destruction and misery are in their ways: And the way
> of peace have they not known: There is no fear of God

before their eyes. Now we know that what things soever the law saith, it saith to them who are under the law: that every mouth may be stopped, and all the world may become guilty before God. Therefore by the deeds of the law there shall no flesh be justified in his sight: for by the law is the knowledge of sin. (Romans 3:9–20)

Here are scriptures in Romans that give us a reason for the law; it was to show man what a desperate condition he was in. The law was good but could not make man good. It shows that the world is guilty before God and that no flesh could be justified in His sight by the deeds of the law. By the law is the knowledge of sin. Before Moses, sin was in the world, but sin was not imputed against man because there was no law. It was given to show man what was right, but man could never do all that was right.

Those under the law had to keep all the law. If they offend in one point, they were guilty in all points. The Bible says Jesus came to fulfill the law by dying on the cross for our sins.

- Luke 24:44: And Jesus said unto them, These are the words which I spake unto you, while I was yet with you, that all things must be fulfilled, which were written in the law of Moses, and in the prophets, and in the psalms, concerning me.
- Acts 13:39: And by him all that believe are justified from all things, from which ye could not be justified by the law of Moses.
- James 2:10: For whosoever shall keep the whole law, and yet offend in one point, he is guilty of all.
- James 2:11: For he that said, Do not commit adultery, said also, Do not kill. Now if thou commit no adultery, yet if thou kill, thou art become a transgressor of the law.
- Galatians 3:24: Wherefore the law was our schoolmaster to bring us unto Christ, that we might be justified by faith.

- Galatians 3:25: But after that faith is come, we are no longer under a schoolmaster.
- Romans 7:7: What shall we say then? Is the law sin? God forbid. Nay, I had not known sin, but by the law: for I had not known lust, except the law had said, Thou shalt not covet.
- Romans 8:1–4: There is therefore now no condemnation to them which are in Christ Jesus, who walk not after the flesh, but after the Spirit. For the law of the Spirit of life in Christ Jesus hath made me free from the law of sin and death. For what the law could not do, in that it was weak through the flesh, God sending his own Son in the likeness of sinful flesh, and for sin, condemned sin in the flesh: That the righteousness of the law might be fulfilled in us, who walk not after the flesh, but after the Spirit.

We see the purpose of the law in just these few scriptures. The law showed mankind how desperately they needed a savior. The law is the strength of sin. For where sin abounded, grace did much more abound. Grace is not really understood without the law. Now, we are not under the law but under grace. The Bible teaches that without the shedding of blood, there is no remission of sin. If you think that putting yourself under the law is pleasing to God, think again; those who put themselves under the law are under a curse.

The Law Brings a Curse

> For as many as are of the works of the law are under the curse; for it is written, "Cursed *is* everyone who does not continue in all things which are written in the book of the law, to do them." (Galatians 3:10)

You have become estranged from Christ, you who *attempt to* be justified by law; you have fallen from grace. (Galatians 5:4)

We Need a Savior and Must Be Born Again

In the beginning, God created man in His own image and likeness and for His pleasure to love and to have a relationship with. God gave man dominion and authority over all earth and to rule over all animals.

Luke 3:38 tells us that Adam was the son of God created from the dust of the ground. Adam was told he could eat freely from all the trees of the garden except for the Tree of the Knowledge of Good and Evil. Once God gave His word to man, He could not break it. So when man ate from the forbidden tree, he died spiritually and began to die physically. When Adam gave in to the words of Satan, Satan became the god of this world and the whole earth and all creation was cursed and corrupted.

God is a just God. Despite what many people believe about Him, He does not do whatever He wants to do. He is sovereign in the sense of being supreme over all creation. But God has limited himself by His own words, and He cannot lie. God knows that the only way for man to be redeemed back to Himself is for his sin to be paid for by a perfect man without sin. But that man had to be born into the world so He would have legal rights here. God could not legally come down and work in the earth without man's permission because He gave His word that man would have authority on earth.

In the Old Testament, men and women were inspired by the Holy Spirit to write down His Word and keep it. After many people came in-line with God's Word, it was time for the Word to become flesh and dwell with mankind. When Jesus was born of a virgin woman, He became the Son of man though He was the Son of God. That man would have to be perfect and keep all the law. That perfect man was Jesus Christ, who was born to take away the sins of the world.

The Word says He bore our sins in His body on the tree that we being dead to sin should live unto righteousness, and by His stripes, we were healed. The Word says that by one man's (Adam's) disobedience, many were made sinners, and by one man's (Jesus's) obedience, many were made righteous. We had no choice because we were made sinners by Adam's act of disobedience. But we now have a choice to be made righteous by believing in Jesus.

The Word says we believe with our hearts that he died for our sins and God raised Him from the dead; thus, we are made righteous and we confess with our mouths unto salvation. When this occurs, the Holy Spirit comes into our hearts and we become new creations. We're born again, and we become children of God, who now is our Father. We are given a great salvation that includes exceedingly great and precious promises. It is our responsibility to find out what this great grace or great salvation is all about and receive it by faith.

> Therefore being justified by faith, we have peace with God through our Lord Jesus Christ. By whom also we have access by faith into this grace wherein we stand, and rejoice in hope of the glory of God. (Romans 5:1–2)

> Grace and peace be multiplied unto you through the knowledge of God, and of Jesus our Lord, According as his divine power hath given unto us all things that pertain unto life and godliness, through the knowledge of him that hath called us to glory and virtue: Whereby are given unto us exceeding great and precious promises: that by these ye might be partakers of the divine nature, having escaped the corruption that is in the world through lust. (2 Peter 1:2–4)

Grace to you and peace from God the Father and our Lord Jesus Christ, who gave Himself for our sins, that He might deliver us from this present evil age, according to the will of our God and Father, to whom *be* glory forever and ever. Amen. (Galatians 1:3–5)

We are justified by faith and have peace with God. He will never reject us, leave us, or forsake us. Grace is accessed by faith wherein we stand. Even grace and peace are multiplied through the knowledge of God. His divine power has given us exceedingly great and precious promises that by these we might partake of His divine nature. We are not just mere men and women anymore; we are children of the most high God. Let's find out what God has given us and access it by faith.

Have you received the baptism of the Holy Spirit mentioned in the book of Acts?

But ye shall receive power, after that the Holy Ghost is come upon you: and ye shall be witnesses unto me both in Jerusalem, and in all Judaea, and in Samaria, and unto the uttermost part of the earth. (Acts 1:8)

There are many scriptures in the book of Acts that testify of this very important gift God wants all His children to have and for them to exercise every day. I cannot imagine not being able to speak in tongues every day.

God bless you.
Sincerely,
Roger Nimmo

About the Author

Denise, my first wife, passed away in 2013. We had four sons—Joshua, Daniel, Caleb, and Joseph. Daniel died when he was five weeks old due to a heart issue. Joseph does construction work and lives in Oklahoma City; he has two sons, Rocco and Sampson.

Joshua is married to Jennifer. They live in Dallas and own an architecture firm. They have two sons, Gabriel and Luke. Caleb is a colonel in the US Air Force and lives in Alexandria, Virginia. He is stationed at the Pentagon. He is married to Laura and they have three sons—Caden, Chase, and Aiden—and one daughter—Lilly.

I am a retired public high school science teacher who has studied the evidence for creation vs. evolution for years. I think the theory of evolution is fake science; it has produced horrible fruit in the world and much unbelief and hardness of hearts in many Christians.

I am married to the sweetest woman I know, the love of my life— Luann Nimmo

Printed in the United States
By Bookmasters